AMAZING AND EXTRAORDINARY FACTS

# SCOTLAND

# SCOTLAND

Douglas Skelton

RP

RYDON
PUBLISHING

A Rydon Publishing Book
35 The Quadrant
Hassocks
West Sussex
BN6 8BP
www.rydonpublishing.co.uk
www.rydonpublishing.com

First published by Rydon Publishing in 2017

ISBN: 978-1-910821-14-5

Printed in Poland by BZ Graf

# CONTENTS

# INTRODUCTION

Scotland is a small country, covering an area of around 31,510 miles. Of course, if you flattened it out it would be much, MUCH larger, for in Scotland, hills and mountains are like pubs in Old Glasgow – always another couple around the corner.

Then there are the islands, almost 800 of them, large and small, habited and uninhabited (apart from sea birds). And there are rivers and lochs – one lake – and yet more hills and valleys and mountains.

Yes, it's a small country, with a population of around 5.3 million. Compare that to the 54.7 million people crammed into the 50,085 square miles of England and you can understand why we have so much space.

There is no such thing as a true Scot, for we are a mongrel race. The Picts gave way to the Celtic Scots from Ireland and the Britons, then came the Normans and the Vikings. And the Romans, of course, although they made limited progress in the harsh land and even harsher climate of northern Britain.

Small country, small population – but Scotland has had a massive impact on the world. The people have migrated, many voluntarily, others forced by landowners who wanted the land on which they had lived for generations to raise sheep. They took with them their stories and traditions and music, integrating with new societies but always retaining a taste of their homeland.

Scots have also helped create modern life. Innovators ushered in the Industrial Revolution, invented technology and made medical breakthroughs. Scottish engineers are famed across the globe.

It is a land of division. Highland and Lowland – a fault line running from Arran in the west to Stonehaven in the North East delineates the two. It can't be seen but its effect has had lasting impact on the nation's culture. East and West – a friendly rivalry between its two great cities, Glasgow and Edinburgh. Edinburgh is the most recent of the nation's capitals but Glasgow was its throbbing industrial heart. Politics and religion – sometimes linked, often bitter, and too readily led to war.

Scottish history has been called 'the long brawl' and that is, unfortunately, accurate. Clan wars, family feuds, invasions of – and by – England have all led to major battles and smaller skirmishes. There is not a section of the Scottish mainland that is not stained by the blood of its people and the enemies of the day.

Nevertheless, the culture survives. The bagpipe, the tartan, the haggis are all archetypal images of Scotland. And yet, none of them likely originated here.

This book explores the long brawl and the culture surrounding it, celebrating the many characters, both well-known and unknown, who populate the annals of Alba. Along the way you will find entries on the food, the sporting heritage and darker tales of murder most foul.

*Douglas Skelton*
Ayrshire, 2017

# CULTURE

**The clan, bagpipes, kilt and the tartan are all typically Scottish. Or are they?**

## We are family
*The beginnings of the clan system*

The notion of the Clan was, like many things typically Scottish, imported. When the Romans withdrew, Scotland was divided into five different races – the Picts of the north, the Britons of Strathclyde, Saxons in the south east, the Attacotti in the west and finally the invading Scots from Ireland.

Around 500 AD, the story goes, three brothers, the sons of Erc, the king of Irish Dalriada, invaded the west from across the Irish Sea. The brothers – Fergus, Angus and Lorne – based themselves on the rock of Dunadd in Argyll and established a tribal system based on families and associations of families. The leader was the father and the tribe was his children, or *cleann,* or *clanna.*

At its heart, a clan is a collection of families who accept one common ancestor. As time wore on, some clans invented fantasies about their inception and their founder. In 1587, in a bid to establish some kind of order, the Roll of the Clans was established.

The concept grew, patriarchal in nature although with loyalty to the mother's line, but not every member was a direct descendant of the founding father. As the idea of surnames took hold, many clan members took the clan name as their own. The truth was that many clanspeople had no blood connection to their chief whatsoever but were part of the larger whole, offering kinship, fellowship and often much-needed protection, there being safety in numbers. Other, smaller, families became attached to the larger groups and were called *Septs.* For the more men the clan chief could call on, the stronger he was.

The western clans were of Celtic or even Norse descent. The eastern clans were mainly derived from an influx of Anglo-Norman families. For instance, the Norman family

La Frèzelière became Fraser, the de Brus family became Bruce and the Fitzalans the Stewarts.

Naturally, they fought with each other, formed alliances, betrayed, usurped and stole. Clan warfare was a way of life and some even grew to oppose the ruling monarch. This led to the MacDonalds, the self-proclaimed Lords of the Isles, being stripped of their titles in 1493, the attempts to extirpate (destroy) the outlawed Clan Gregor and the need for an oath of loyalty that culminated in the bloodshed of Glencoe.

The barbarous reprisals after the battle of Culloden in 1746 and the Highland Clearances, with many Scots being betrayed by the people they thought were their leaders and protectors, all but destroyed the clan system. However, the romanticism of the 19th century, led by Sir Walter Scott, paved the way for a revival, although threaded through with rose-tinted memories.

The clan societies of today keep the traditions and stories and heritage of the system very much alive across the globe.

## GAINING A FOOTHOLD

*It was the invading Scots from Ireland who settled on a former Iron Age hillfort rock outcrop in the middle of boggy land near Kilmartin in Argyll called Dunadd. Here they established the capital of the kingdom of Dalriada.*

*This historic site boasts a number of rock carvings, including a boar, a basin cut out of solid rock and an inscription in the ancient Irish Ogham script which no one has properly translated.*

*Dalriadic kings put their foot down in order to rule*

*There are also two carved footprints and it is believed this was used during coronation ceremonies of the old Dalriadic kings to symbolise his foothold on the land.*

# An instrument of war
*For centuries, Scots have been led into battle by the bagpipes*

The skirl of the pipes over the heather, the lone piper high above Edinburgh Castle bringing the Military Tattoo to a close, the kilted bands marching in formation – there can be nothing that brings Scotland more to mind.

It's a shame that the bagpipes weren't devised here.

There are forms of bagpipes across the globe – Ireland, of course, Spain, Hungary, Germany, Italy – while history is peppered with references to variations of the instrument. The ancient Romans had their own version and even the Emperor Nero was reputed to have been a dab hand with the bag and sticks.

Of course, whether or not the distinctive sound of the pipes is music is subject to individual tastes. While some feel the need to rally to arms and vanquish a foe, others feel the need to vanquish the piper. One ancient writer likened the sound of the pipes to 'dogs in distress.'

In Scotland, the pipes became a weapon of war and may have been used to relay instructions during battle, very much in the manner of a bugle.

The first mention of the bagpipes being used to urge armies to slaughter one another was in 1627, but the likelihood is that the instrument was deployed even earlier. Every clan had their piper and they were honoured, for they could not only instil bloodlust but also move the hardy Highlander to tears. The piper had to be musically gifted and extremely brave, for he had to stand alone and unarmed as the battle raged around him.

The MacCrimmons, pipers to the MacLeod clan, were reputedly the greatest exponents of the art. The origin of this family has been debated – one theory held that they originated from Italy, another that they were of Norse descent – but their name has been attached to fine piping for centuries.

One, according to legend, even composed a *pibroch*, as the music for the pipes is called, while he watched the village of an enemy burn in retaliation for the murder of his brother.

The instruments used in battle became a matter of law in 1746. Angus piper James Reid had been with Lord Ogilvy's Regiment, fighting for Bonnie Prince Charlie at Culloden, but was captured and taken to York to face trial. His defence was that, although he had marched with the Jacobite army, he had never fired a shot nor swung a sword against the Government forces. The jury accepted the argument and recommended mercy but the judge was not in a forgiving mood. He said that Highland armies never marched without a piper and it followed that the bagpipes were an 'instrument of war.'

Piper Reid was hanged, drawn and quartered with 23 other Jacobites.

The tradition of the piper leading Scots regiments into battle continued within the British Army and there are many tales of bravery as the men played in the midst of gunfire and death.

During World War I, the piper was instrumental in stiffening the

*Pipers led troops into battle*

resolve of Scottish troops' advancing across the killing fields. The unarmed piper was an easy target for the enemy and many were killed.

One of the lucky ones was Daniel Laidlaw. Born in Berwickshire, he was 40 years old when he helped galvanise the battle-weary men to push forward at Loos in September 1915. He mounted the parapet of the trench and began to play his pipes. The men rallied and surged across the battlefield. Piper Laidlaw continued to play even after being wounded and was awarded the Victoria Cross for his valour. He was only one of two pipers awarded his country's highest medal of honour, the other being a Canadian.

## WHAT'S THAT BUNDLE OF STICKS?

*Following the failure of Bonnie Prince Charlie's attempt to seize the throne in 1745/6, many things Highland were outlawed or discouraged. The bagpipes, although not prohibited by law, were certainly frowned upon, for they were a symbol of the martial nature of the Scot that the Hanoverian Government wished to stamp out. However, the Duke of Cumberland himself had witnessed the preparations made by those Highland Regiments fighting for his father, King George II. He asked about the 'bundles of sticks' and was told that they were the bagpipes and that without them the Highlander would be of no use in battle.*

## THE D-DAY PIPER

*By World War II, pipers were ordered to remain very much in the rear during action.*

*However, on D–Day in June 1944, Bill Millin was part of Lord Lovat's Commandos when he was ordered to play the men ashore. Millin pointed out that regulations forbade it but Lovat said, 'That's the English War Office. You and I are Scottish and so it doesn't apply.'*

*Piper Bill Millin's statue at what was Sword Beach, Normandy*

*Millin, the only man in his company to wear the kilt (one worn by his father in Flanders), waded ashore. Amazingly, he survived – because the German sharp-shooters thought him mad and left him alone.*

*In 2009 he was awarded the French Croix d'Honneur and there is now a statue of him on the site of Sword Beach, a lone piper, kilt swinging, playing amid the carnage of war.*

# Battle of the Clans
*Bloodletting was pre-planned*

Today the North Inch of Perth is a quiet park, a stretch of green grass and trees on the banks of the Tay. But in 1396 it was a marshy area that became the scene of a bloody clan battle with a difference.

The violent feud between the Clans Cameron and Chattan had become ever-more brutal and it was finally decided that the matter would be ended by a gladiatorial fight to the death between the king and his courtiers.

King Robert III (c.1337/1406) decreed the hostilities would be waged in Perth and he would watch from a gilded summerhouse at nearby Blackfriars Monastery. The winners would be honoured and the losers, if still alive, would be pardoned.

The exact date of the clash is debated. Sir Walter Scott (1771–1832) said it was on Palm Sunday but other historians favour a date in September. Even the clans involved has been disputed, such is the vague nature of sections of Scottish history.

Each of the combatants were armed with claymore (the great two-handed sword of the clansman), dagger, bow and targe (the small, round shield favoured by the Highlander).

The Inch was barricaded on three sides, the Tay delineating the fourth edge of the field. The men marched through the town with great ceremony, their pipers ahead of them, while the crowds pressed into the barriers, eager to see blood spilled.

However, Clan Chattan only

*Clan battles could be bloody affairs*

had 29 men, whether due to sickness or failure of nerve is not known, and were unwilling to proceed being outnumbered. No one in the opposition was inclined to sit the battle out so an appeal was made to the crowd for any man willing to come forward and fight for a fee. Amazingly, one man did so and was granted half a gold crown and the promise of a pension should he survive.

Battle commenced with the famed Highland Charge, spurred on by the inspirational words of their bards and the blood-stirring sound of the pipes. Each side galloped across the marshy ground and met in the middle in a clash of steel. They hacked, they lunged, they parried and blocked. Men died or were wounded. There was a pause in the fighting and the pipers recalled the ambulant combatants for a breather, but then they surged again.

In the end, Clan Chattan had eleven men still standing, while the Camerons were reduced to a single fighter. Faced with insurmountable odds, he decided that discretion was the better part of valour and swam across the Tay to safety. It is said that he returned to his family home and was ostracised for his lack of nerve. He later killed himself.

Victory was declared for the Chattans. And the local volunteer, often said to be Henry Smith, or Hal O' The Wynd, equipped himself well in the melee and lived to tell of it.

Today, the site of the slaughter is marked by a somewhat unimpressive plaque set in a brick pillar beside the park.

---

## THE CRY TO BATTLE
*The modern word slogan has come to mean little more than a catchy phrase to sell products. But to the Scottish Clansman it was the* **sluagh-ghairm,** *a battle cry. (In Gaelic,* **sluagh** *means army and* **ghairm** *yell.)*

*And clans each had their own call to arms. It could be a phrase, a location in their lands or merely the repetition of their name. Granted many sound better in their native Gaelic but here are a few, in English to make it easier.*

*For the Camerons it was 'Sons of the hounds come hither for flesh.' The powerful Campbells merely cried out 'Cruachan!' (The mountain on Loch Awe). The Douglas cry was simply, 'A Douglas! A Douglas!' The Homes were similar – 'A Home! A Home!' The Setons were playful with their name, bellowing 'Set on! Set on!' The McAlpins exhorted warriors to 'Remember the death of McAlpin!' The Macdougalls surged into battle with 'Victory or death!*

# The best plaid schemes
*The tartan myth*

The tartan is another iconic part of culture that is not strictly Scottish. Fragments of tartan cloth dating to around 1200 BC were found on mummies in western China, while the actual weaving secret may have come to Scotland from Ireland with the Dalriadic Scots.

The word 'Tartan' is not even Scottish. It is most likely derived from the French *tiretaine*, which was a mixture of wool and linen and did not relate to the actual pattern. The Scots would have used the word for speckled – *breacan*, It could also mean multi-coloured. A length of tartan cloth which could be wrapped around the body and fastened with a belt was called a *plaid*, and when Scots migrated to the Americas this word became synonymous with tartan.

An early mention of the tartan comes in 1538 when we learn that King James V (1512–1542) bought a quantity of 'Helan Tertans' for his French wife, Mary of Guise

(1515–1560). The oldest known tangible example is the Falkirk Tartan, a simple two-colour weave dating back to the third century, which was found in an earthenware jar close to the Antonine Wall.

The association of individual patterns to clans is not as traditional as the world has been led to believe. Certainly the Celts here and in their homelands on the continent were fond of vivid colours and adornments. They favoured stripes and even simple chequered patterns.

Some patterns – or setts – were associated with a few Highland families around the 16th century but it was far from widespread. Most clans were identified in battle by something other than the pattern of their dress – a flower, a leaf, a ribbon that could be pinned to their cap.

What would associate clans, or areas, with a particular sett may have been down to the men and women who made the clothes. The weavers would supply the cloth for their village or district using locally available, natural colourings and dyes and that, by extension, might mean that certain colours and perhaps designs became the uniform of their clan. But it was by no means widespread.

By the time of the disastrous Jacobite Rebellion of 1745/46, the tartan had become very popular among the Highlanders but the rising, following the slaughter at Culloden, led to it being proscribed by law along with other symbols of the Gael's way of life, at least for ordinary folk. The law did not apply to nobility or, importantly, the military.

In the 19th century, attempts were made to restore some kind of national pride and the wearing of the tartan and the kilt crept into vogue. It was Sir Walter Scott and his involvement in the 1822 grand visit of King George IV to Edinburgh that helped turn tartan into the global marketing brand it is today. Highland chiefs were urged to attend functions in traditional garb and even the fat little King was persuaded to don a kilt. Scott also used tartan in his hugely successful novels as he romanticised his country's history and culture.

*Contrary to myth, tartan designs were not associated with individual clans*

Queen Victoria and Prince Albert were very fond of Scott's idea of Scotland and favoured the tartan during their visits. It was the Prince himself who designed the Balmoral Tartan, and drenched their fairy tale Highland hideaway in drapes, furniture and floor coverings bearing his design. That particular sett can still only be worn by the royal family, with permission from the Queen, and her personal piper.

## DYED IN THE WOOL

*Clan weavers used natural sources for their dyes and the colours common to their fabrics were dictated by what resources they could locate locally. The material had to be treated with a mordant to fix the dye to the wool and often this meant soaking it in urine.*

*Black could be obtained from Alder tree bark or dock root, blue from elderberry while white and dark lichens could supply light or dark crimson. Green came from broom or whin Bark and yellow from bog myrtle, bracken root or St John's wort.*

# The Tartan conmen
*Two fascinating brothers helped create the myth of clan tartans*

Charles Edward Stuart – better known as Bonnie Prince Charlie (1720–1788) – had only one child, an illegitimate daughter named Clementina.

But that didn't stop two brothers from convincing many in 19th century Scots society that they were descended from the tragic royal dynasty. Styling themselves John and Charles Edward Sobieski Stolberg Stuart, they fabricated a story that the prince had fathered a son in 1773, after his marriage by proxy at the age of 51 to the 18-year-old Princess Louise. The child was taken from Italy to England to avoid any unpleasant encounters with the Hanoverian authorities.

The name of the Royal Naval officer who agreed to raise the child changed over the time of their telling of the tale but finally they settled on John Carter Allen, who rose to the rank of Admiral. His son, Thomas Allen, also joined the Royal Navy, married and had two sons.

The brothers arrived in Scotland in the early 1820s and, although they offered nothing to substantiate their claims, they were charming and managed to pull off the con trick.

Thanks to Sir Walter Scott, and others, as well as the pomp and circumstance generated for the visit of George IV's Edinburgh visit of 1822, a romantic flame regarding

*Tartans have long been associated with individual clans but it's a myth*

Scotland's culture had been kindled. Noble families clasped the brothers to their collective bosom and they enjoyed a fine life. The chief of Clan Fraser was so taken with their story that he offered them a home for a time on an island on the River Beauly, where they took to being fashioned 'the Princes.' They also adopted the name Sobieski, after the surname of their Polish 'great-grandmother', Maria Clementina Sobieska.

They claimed to have in their possession ancient documents once owned by their 'real' grandfather, Bonnie Prince Charlie, which detailed the tartans relating to the Scottish clans. Only one document was ever shown, however, and even then it was a copy.

Nevertheless, their word was taken at face value and the brothers wrote the *Vestiarium Scoticum,* a sumptuous volume bound in red leather and purporting to show all the clan tartans, both Highland and Lowland. It was impressively illustrated by Charles, reproduced thanks to a new system developed by the Smith brothers in Mauchline, Ayrshire. For the first time people could actually see the various setts attributed to the clans.

But it was all bogus. A few people raised doubts – Sir Walter Scott was never convinced by their stories – but the idea was embraced by society, not to mention weavers who saw a way to capitalise on the whole notion. The book was subsequently used by other writers to help compound the myth of clan tartans.

It wasn't until late in the 20th century that it was revealed to be an almost complete fraud. Some of the tartans may well have been genuine but most of them were devised by the artist brother, Charles.

The brothers did not produce the book for great financial gain but merely to cement their position in society. Sir Walter Scott, however, suggested that the real movers behind it were the men of the weaving industry, who saw a way to make a buck. And they made out like bandits.

Eventually the brothers were exposed and fell from grace. John Sobieski Stuart fashioned himself the Count d'Albanie until his death in 1872. His brother then took up the title but died eight years later.

Charlatans they may have been but they are two of the least known yet most fascinating characters in Scottish history.

## KILT COMPLEX

*The Scottish kilt may not be as ancient as we think. It has its roots in the* **phileig-mhor,** *the great wrap or belted plaid, the long fabric wrapped and folded around the body, that could also be used as a cloak and as bedding when sleeping rough. It is first noted in the 16th century, although could have been in use earlier. It is unlikely that they were tartan.*

*It became more common in the 17th and 18th centuries, when tartan setts did begin to manifest themselves, although many were of single colours to allow the wearer to blend more easily into the landscape.*

## HEMLINE REDUCTION

*The creation of the* **phileig-beag,** *the small kilt, has been attributed to English mill owner Thomas Rawlinson, who in 1720 issued it to his Scottish workers to prevent them from getting their bulkier clothing caught in the machinery.*

*It was later adopted by the Highland regiments when the style of uniform jacket changed to a tighter fitting garment and the longer 'plaid' simply didn't fit.*

*George IV, during his visit to Edinburgh in 1822, sported the small, or walking, kilt that is now more common at ceilidhs and weddings.*

# Minding their language
*A taste of Gaelic*

Gaelic was yet another part of Scottish culture that originated in Ireland and came across the water with the Dalriadic Scots in the 4th and 5th centuries. As they moved, the language spread to supplant the Pictish tongue.

It never gained a serious foothold in southern areas of Scotland, though, where people began to speak a kind of Middle English known as Lallans or simply Scots, as exemplified by the poetry of Robert Burns.

Despite strenuous efforts to revive interest, it is believed that just over one per cent of the population speak Gaelic, which is recognised as indigenous but not an official language of the British Isles, although it does remain the first language for many people in the Hebrides. Many road signs and railway station signs carry both the English and Gaelic versions of the place names.

The first thing to know about Gaelic is that there are only eighteen letters in the alphabet – it does not use the letters J, K, Q, V, W, X, Y or Z. Different sounds are created by accented letters or letters brought together.

The language spoken today by the majority of Scots is English, although dialects have been influenced not just by the Gaelic, but also the language of the Celts, the Norse and the French.

And Gaelic words have crept into common English usage across the world. 'Bard' for 'poet' is an obvious example, but bog is derived from the Gaelic pronounced *pok,* which means 'soft.'

The term 'smashing', meaning pleasing, probably comes from *'s math sin,* which means 'it is good.'

Cairn comes from *càrn,* galore is from *gu leor,* meaning 'enough', and *gob* means beak.

A *peata* was a tame animal and from that we get today's pet. The MacIntosh coat was derived from the name of its originator but his name was from *Mac an Tòisich,* meaning 'son of the chieftan'.

*Many road signs carry both the English and Gaelic place names*

Shindig was originally *sinteag* and meant to jump around, while the word 'pillion' comes from the Gaelic for saddle bag, *pillean.* A banshee, the *bean-sithe* of the Gaelic Scots, was a woman of the fairy mound (also common to Irish Gaelic). Bun, as in 'cute or firm buns', comes from the same word in Gaelic which means bottom. When you twig to something you understand it, from the word *tuig.*

---

### WHAT'S IN A NAME?

*Many place names in Scotland have a hidden meaning and are derived from either their Pictish, Gaelic or Anglo-Saxon origins – or sometimes a mixture of them all. The cities of Aberdeen, Glasgow, Edinburgh, Dundee, Inverness and Perth all have meaning in their names (respectively, the Mouth of the Don, Dear Green Place, Fort of the Rock Face, Fort of Daig or Dark Hill, Mouth of the River Ness and Place of the Thicket).*

*Names with 'Aber' generally mean a river mouth, as in Aberfoyle, from the Pictish* **aber**

*Some say that Edinburgh means Fort of the Rock Place*

*which means confluence and the Gaelic phuill which means pool.*

*The prefix 'Pit' is also Pictish, for portion, so Pitlochry means 'piece of land by the stones' thanks to the addition of the Gaelic* **cloichreach** *stones. The stones were stepping stones across the nearby River Tummel. The word* **dun** *is Gaelic for 'hill' or 'fort' and* **barr** *is 'height' so Dunbar was the 'fort on the height'. Kin is from the Gaelic* **ceann**, *head, and when joined with the word for pine wood,* **ghiuthsaich**, *we have Kingussie – at the head of the pine wood. And one of the shortest place names in the world – Ae, a river, forest and village in the Borders – comes from the Norse* **aa**, *for water.*

## RAP TAKES FLYTE

*Rapping is an art form which has been honed by African-Americans. However, it may have been taken across the Atlantic by a group of men Scotland is not proud of – the slave owner.*

*Flyting was a Norse import that hit the big time in Scotland during the 15th and 16th centuries as a form of entertainment.*

*It involved rival poets lambasting each other with a series of insulting, and often profane, verses. It received royal approval when both James IV and V encouraged court poets, the* **makaris**, *to engage in such contests and even took part themselves.*

*The most famous example from this period is the 'The Flyting of Dunbar and Kennedy', an epic battle between poets William Dunbar and Walter Kennedy witnessed by James IV.*

# On the trail
*Cattle driving in the Highlands*

The cattle drive was for many years a staple of western films and TV shows. However, the heyday of the great US drives lasted only around 20 years. In Scotland, the era of the drover lasted far longer but has not been mythologised in literature or drama. They did not round the cattle up by horse but pushed them on foot, from the hills and straths (valleys) and islands of the north to the markets in the south and from there to the bellies of the growing population and the military.

The black cattle of the Highlands, like the people themselves, were a hardy breed. The herds live on in the hugely photogenic long-haired Highland cows, both brown and black.

The men whose business it was to get them to market, or trysts, were independent workers and as tough as the land itself. Come droving season, late summer into autumn, they would be either hired to push the herds south to market,

or would gather the beasts door-to-door from the settlements and crofts of the north.

These herds could vary in size from 100 to 2,000 head. The tough drovers were well prepared for the rigours ahead. Rivers had to be crossed, ravines skirted and rustlers – the *caterans* of the north and *reivers* of the south – had to be fought off, for cattle-lifting was a way of life both in the Highlands and the Lowlands. The drovers were well-armed and necessarily so, for the reiving bands could be ruthless. Their routes criss-crossed the country and stuck as much as they could to fertile lands where the feeding was good but there were times they had to climb mountain passes and down again.

The men lived on a diet of oats, either heated as porridge or taken with cold water, and onions. They would also have mixed in some blood harvested from the necks of cattle in their charge. Of course, there would be whisky.

The herds could travel 150 to 200 miles, to the markets of Falkirk and Crieff. The big cattle trysts meant profit not only for the cattle dealers, for they attracted money-lenders and entertainers and purveyors of pleasure who set up stalls and touted their own wares.

For centuries, when war raged at regular intervals between Scotland and England, trade was banned. Following James VI's accession to the English throne in 1603, a free trade agreement was established and the cattle could be marketed over the border, where the big money was. The heyday was during the 18th and 19th century when the navy demanded a seemingly endless supply of salt beef to maintain the men during incessant wars with France.

But progress, as it always does, began to outstrip the centuries-old practice. The black cattle were increasingly replaced by sheep as their Highland Lordships cleared their former clansmen from the land. Steamships docked in the bays and carried the beasts away. And then came the railways.

Droving continued in a small way until the early part of the 20th century but then it died out and the drover himself became as extinct as the black cattle he once herded.

*The Highland cow is descended from the hardy black cattle*

## THE EXTORTION RACKET THAT GAVE THE WORLD A WORD

***Raiders promising to leave herds alone if the owners paid them a tribute led to a new word entering the English language. This was a robbers' tax and the name given to it was black-mail. It was common among the Highland caterans and the Border reivers.***

*The theories of the origins of the term are varied. One is simply that it means 'nefarious rent.' Another that it is derived from the Gaelic blathaich (to protect) and mal (from the Norse word for agreement). Another is that it was a black rent, distinct from the white rent that was paid in silver.*

# MAKERS OF HISTORY

A few of the people who have made their mark in Scotland's history.

## Snakes and monsters
*St Patrick and St Columba*

With all that has been imported from Ireland into Scottish culture, it's only fitting that we send something back. And it's only their patron saint!

St Patrick may have been born around *c.*485 AD near Dumbarton on the Clyde, and at the age of 16, he was kidnapped by slave traders and carried off to pagan Ireland. He escaped but decided to return as a missionary, first converting the clan chiefs. Along the way he banished all the snakes on the emerald isle – a neat trick as there weren't any there to begin with.

Curiously, patron saint though he is, he was never officially canonised.

After St Patrick exported himself to Ireland to spread the word, an Irish missionary returned the favour and crossed the Irish Sea to convert the Scots.

Of royal blood, Columba (521–597) – also known as *Colmkil* or *Columcille* – left Ireland blaming himself for causing the slaughter of 3,000 men in a family feud. He had been accused of stealing a book of psalms and he appealed to his clan, the O'Neills, for help. He arrived on the tiny island of Iona in 563 where he set up his first church, then set out to spread the word across Scotland.

He has even been associated with the Loch Ness Monster, for according to legend he had an encounter with the beastie in 565 AD. His chronicler, Adamnan, wrote a century later that Columba was crossing the loch when he saw men tending to a man who had been attacked by some kind of water creature. He sent one of his followers to help but the monster reared up and attacked. Columba was having none of that and roared at the creature to retreat at once. Amazingly, the beast did.

And that is the first written mention of what would become the legendary Nessie.

### PILATE SCHEME

*In Fortingall in Perthshire there is a yew tree reputed to be 5,000 years old. If only it could talk, for it would be able to confirm or deny that Pontius Pilate (c.20 BC to 36 AD) was born there.*

*The story goes that, although Romans didn't invade Britain until 43–80 AD, they did visit much earlier. The Emperor Augustus sent envoys to strike treaties with the major tribes and one ended up in Glen Lyon to cosy up to the locals. He fell for a local warlord's daughter and they had a son, Pontius Pilate, who was raised in Rome.*

*However, the story may be a joke created by a local landowner and his playboy friends in the 19th century.*

## What bloody man is that?
*The real Macbeth*

Shakespeare was never one for historical accuracy, but with his bloody tale of Macbeth he really went to town.

There was a king of that name but he wasn't quite the bloodthirsty, henpecked monster of the play. Mac Bethad mac Findlaích (1005–1057) was the *Mormaer*, essentially a steward or earl, of Moray in the north-east.

Yes, he did seize the throne from the weak and unpopular Duncan, who had been king for six years, but it was in battle, near Elgin in 1040, and not by murder most foul. Macbeth had a solid claim to the throne. At his side was his wife, Gruach, who was also descended from royalty.

He was a good king, reigning the northern part of Scotland, or Alba, for seventeen years. He kept the peace, he encouraged Christianity, he made laws. He defended his kingdom in the north from the Norsemen of Orkney and Duncan's sons who ruled Strathclyde in the south.

It was in 1057 that one of these sons – Malcolm – headed north with an army bolstered by the ruler of Northumbria and the English king Edward the Confessor. Macbeth's forces met them at Lumphanan, to the west of Aberdeen, and he was killed in battle. He was buried on Iona in the *Rèilig Odhrain*, St Oran's Shrine, the burial ground of 48 kings and chiefs.

His step-son, Lulach the fool (*c.*1030–1058), was crowned king but he survived only four months before Malcolm's forces struck again and he was killed at Strathbogie. His body joined his step father's in the *Rèilig Odhrain*.

So, there were no witches, no Birnam Wood heading to Dunsinane, no ghosts. Shakespeare was trying to curry favour with

*Shakespeare played fast and loose with the facts in Macbeth*

James I (VI of Scotland) who claimed descent from Banquo. The problem was, Banquo had never existed, except in a dodgy history and even then he's painted as much a villain as Macbeth. The playwright whitewashed the character – and also added the witches. It is they who prophecy that a line of royalty beginning with Banquo would 'stretch out to the crack of doom.' That would've kept James very happy.

There is a Dunsinane, however, and Macbeth did clash there with Malcolm's forces, although it was not decisive. Dunsinnan, the hill of ants, is north east of Perth near the village of Collace and carries the remains of two hill forts. Certainly it is within marching distance of Dunkeld to the north west but there are no historical records of Birnam Wood being uprooted and transported.

---

**THAT PLAY WAS A RIOT**
*'The Scottish Play' is deemed unlucky in theatrical circles. That was certainly true for New Yorkers in 1849 when rival productions spawned a riot that left many dead.*

*American actor Edward Forrest and his British rival William Charles MacReady were already feuding over whose performance was best. On 10 May, 10,000 of Forrest's fans stormed the theatre in which MacReady was playing to show their support for their idol. He escaped but the police chief ordered his men to fire into the crowd. The number of dead varies but it was certainly around 25, with many more wounded.*

---

## The king who helped create Scotland
*Malcolm III brought the kingdoms together*

They called him Malcolm Canmore, from *Ceann* (chief or head*) Mor* (big), and though he may have gained power by bumping off both Macbeth and Lulach in battle, he is the monarch who is, rightly or wrongly, credited with shaping modern Scotland.

He began a royal line that

*The memorial marks where Malcolm Canmore died at Alnwick*

would rule for 230 years. For by taking the throne of Alba and uniting it with that of Strathclyde – not to mention reaching an accommodation with the powerful Earls of Orkney by marrying the widow of the wonderfully named Thorfinn Sigurdsson – he brought a certain amount of stability to the rambunctious country.

Malcolm III (1031–1093) welcomed many refugee Anglo-Saxons nobles from England following the hostile Norman takeover of 1066, which upset the new management in London. His first wife, Ingibjörg, had died so he even married the pious and gentle Margaret of Wessex, herself a member of Anglo-Saxon royalty. However, the influx of new blood did lead to a certain amount of Anglification in the Scottish court. He even abandoned the traditional Gaelic names for his offspring by naming them Edward, Edmund, David and Alexander.

That didn't mean he was of a peaceful mind towards his neighbours to the south, for he led regular incursions into their territory, committing many acts Scots generally prefer to blame on the English. In fact, it was said that he took so many hostages that there was not a house in Scotland that didn't have an English slave.

Finally, in 1072, William the Conqueror took matters into his own hands and rode into Scotland, forcing himself as far as the Tay. At Abernethy, south-east of Perth, the two kings reached an agreement whereby Malcolm paid homage to the English king as his master. It was an act that would haunt the Scots for centuries to come. Malcolm, though, had no intention of keeping the peace and within a few years he was back south again, burning and pillaging.

When an arranged meeting with William Rufus, who had succeeded to the English throne, did not take place, Malcolm returned north in a temper and proceeded to invade Northumbria again. This would be his last taste of war for in 1093, at Alnwick, he was killed. The site of his death, said to be thanks to the thrust of a lance, is marked with a stone cross. His body was carried to Tynemouth but was later recovered and interred in Dunfermline Abbey.

*St Margaret's Chapel, the oldest building in Edinburgh, founded by Malcolm's wife*

## THE PEARL OF SCOTLAND

*Malcolm III's second wife, Margaret (1045–1093), was the opposite of her husband. Where he was warlike, she was gentle, where he was intemperate, she was reasoned. She became known to some as*

*'The Pearl of Scotland.' Among her many good works was a church at Dunfermline and her chapel on Edinburgh's castle rock, which is the oldest building in Edinburgh.*

*When her son Edgar brought her news of her husband's death, she was so grief-stricken that she herself died three days later. She was buried in Dunfermline Abbey and was canonised in 1250. Relics of her body, however, were retained and Mary, Queen of Scots had her head in her possession. Eventually in the care of French Jesuits, it was later lost in the revolution. Mary, of course, had lost hers many years before.*

# The Guardian of Scotland
*The man who cried 'Freedom'*

William Wallace (*c.*1270–1305) loomed large in Scottish history, even before Mel Gibson painted his face blue and cried 'Freedom.' Depending on which side of the border you stood, he was seen as a freedom fighter or a bandit, a hero or a villain, a martyr or a bloodthirsty criminal who got what he deserved.

Curiously, for a man who cast such a giant shadow across the Scottish psyche, very little is actually known about him. Much of the legend comes from an epic poem, *The Wallace* by Blind Harry the Minstrel, a largely hagiographical account of Wallace's life which became the second most read book in Scotland after the Bible.

Even his date and place of birth is debated, with strong cases made for both Elderslie in

*Scottish hero
William Wallace*

Renfrewshire, on the outskirts of Glasgow, and Ellerslie, now part of Kilmarnock in Ayrshire. He was of minor nobility but during the period after the death of Alexander III in 1286 the future of the Scottish throne was debated. The English king Edward I saw the chance to establish a foothold north of the border, and demanded that Scottish nobles sign a treaty of fealty, a document that became known as the Ragman's Roll after the forest of ribbons that dangled from the various seals.

The young Wallace was not one of the signatories and, at some point, managed to kill an English official. Where this occurred, or why, is unclear but Blind Harry states it was because the lord killed his young wife.

Finding himself on the run, he joined up with other rebellious young Scots nobles, including Sir Andrew de Moray, and set about harrying the English whenever and wherever they could, climaxing in the famous victory at Stirling Bridge, when the Scots used the narrow bridge to hem in the enemy and slaughter them. Unfortunately, de Moray was mortally wounded during the battle.

Wallace found himself named a Guardian of Scotland but the English king was far from finished with the troublesome little nation. He personally led an army northwards and clashed with Wallace at Falkirk. This time the English were victorious.

Wallace was again on the run and little is known of his movements, although he may have been in both France and Germany gathering support.

Back home, the Scots nobles were busy doing what Scots nobles did best – looking after themselves. When Wallace returned in 1303 he found that Edward was more or less in control and treating Scotland like an English province. Two years later, he was betrayed.

On 23 August, Wallace stood trial in Westminster Hall, accused of being a traitor who had broken an oath of fealty that he had never actually sworn. He was charged with treason, murder and rapine. There is a plaque near the King's Bench in the hall pointing out the spot that Wallace stood to hear the evidence against him. The trial was a farce and the guilty verdict was a foregone conclusion. The punishment was barbaric, even for those brutal days.

He was dragged to the Tower of London as crowds jeered and threw missiles. From there he was taken to Smithfield where he was hanged, drawn and quartered. His head was placed on a pike over London Bridge, parts of his mutilated body sent for public display at Newcastle, Berwick, Stirling and Perth.

Today, on the wall of St Bartholomew's Church, overlooking the meat market at Smithfield, there is a plaque commemorating 'Sir William Wallace, patriot of Scotland…who fought dauntlessly in defence of his country's liberty.'

As far as is known, Edward never came face-to-face with the man he hated. He was not present in Westminster Hall for the trial nor the execution.

## A SLAP IN THE MENTEITH

*The man who betrayed William Wallace was Sir John Menteith (c.1275–1329), who had made his peace with the English king and been appointed Warden of Dumbarton Castle on the Clyde. Wallace was either sheltering in a barn or in a tavern at Robroyston, on the outskirts of Glasgow, on 5 August when the soldiers took him. Legend tells us that Menteith gave the signal by turning over a bannock on a table. Again, according to tradition, his betrayal was so repugnant that the loch that carries his name is the only one in Scotland that is called by the English 'lake'.*

# The man who would be king
*Robert the Bruce, Scotland's most famous monarch*

Robert I, better known as Robert the Bruce (1274–1329), strides like a lion through history.

Surprisingly, for such a well-known figure, debate rages over his birthplace.

Claims are made for Lochmaben in Dumfries and Galloway and Writtle in Essex. However, the most likely place of his birth was Turnberry Castle in Carrick, on the west coast of Ayrshire. This was the family home of his mother, the remarkable Marjorie of Carrick, who, if legend is to be believed,

*A memorial, erected in 1900, marked the spot where Wallace was betrayed*

held his father prisoner until he agreed to marry her.

The young Bruce supported attempts to place the crown on his grandfather's head. He was, however, a clever political operator who, like other Scots claimants, could switch sides when the need arose. One minute it appeared he was cosying up to Edward I, the next he was staring down the edge of his sword at English forces. He played both ends against the middle and enriched his family in the process.

Finally, after the brutal death of William Wallace, Bruce made his play. The claim to the throne had passed to him on the death of his grandfather. The problem was, there were other claimants, among them John 'The Red' Comyn. Bruce solved that particular problem by murdering him in Greyfriars church in Dumfries.

It was this act of violence that set Bruce on the path to the throne. He had himself crowned at Scone, the ancient capital, but the way ahead was not an easy one, for in the early days he was beset with

defeat and was excommunicated for sacrilege, thanks to committing murder in a holy place. Eventually he had to flee the country, some say to Rathlin Island, off the coast of Antrim, while his wife and children were imprisoned.

On his return following the death of Edward I, he began a guerrilla war against the English and the Scots families who supported them. He rampaged through Buchan, laying waste to everything he touched. He reduced castles to rubble so the English could not use them. Finally, in 1314, Bruce and Edward faced each other over two midsummer days on the field and stream and marshes at Bannockburn. The Scots were outnumbered but Bruce used the topography and the schiltron, blocks of spearmen grouped together with their spears sticking out like the spines of a hedgehog, to murderous effect.

It was Bruce, they say, who drew first blood, killing the heavily armed Sir Henry de Bohun with a blow from his battle axe.

Bannockburn was a famous

victory but the war was not over. It continued until 1328, when Scotland's independence from England was finally recognised. By that time, Edward II (1284–1327) had already been deposed by his wife and her lover and later murdered.

Robert the Bruce, King of Scots, died in his manor at Cardross above the Clyde near Dumbarton. His body was interred at Dunfermline Abbey and the ornate tomb can be seen today, complete with bronze cast of his skull.

His heart was taken from his body and, as per his wishes, taken on a crusade. In Spain, his faithful friend Sir James Douglas and the loyal knights of his escort fought with the Moors. Surrounded and outnumbered, Douglas threw the casket containing the heart into the fray, saying that the king should go first as he had always done, then followed it. The Scots were slaughtered.

Somehow, though, the heart was apparently returned to Scotland and it was buried in the grounds of Melrose Abbey in the Borders.

*The statue of Robert the Bruce at Bannockburn*

## IF AT FIRST…

*Of the many stories attached to Robert the Bruce, the most potent is his encounter with a spider whose attempts to form a web gave him the heart to carry on fighting.*

*It was while his cause was at a low ebb and he was hiding in a hut or a cave – the former perhaps on Rathlin Island, the latter perhaps on the Isle of Arran, or near Dumfries – that he watched the determined arachnid swing from one place to another until it finally succeeded. The spider's example taught him that 'If at first you don't succeed, try, try again…'*

*It's a fine story but in all likelihood was invented during the Victorian era.*

## CAUSE OF DEATH

*For centuries there was debate over the cause of Robert the Bruce's death, with claims that it was leprosy dismissed as propaganda to smear him.*

*The cast of Robert the Bruce's skull*

*However, in 2016, technology allowed a more detailed facial reconstruction to be made from the cast of his skull and it was insisted it showed signs of the disease.*

*There are still many who dismiss the claim, saying that the Bruce was simply worn out and riddled with arthritis, and that the remains of lesions are, in fact, battle scars.*

## A DECLARATION OF INDEPENDENCE

*Scotland's Independence mandate was probably written by Bernand de Linton, the Abbot of Arbroath. It was designed as a plea to the Pope to intercede in the ongoing war.*

*It does, however, contain a warning to the Bruce, that should he ever turn from his path of freeing Scotland from the English yoke he'd be cast out 'as subverter of our rights and of his own' and Scotland would 'choose another king to defend our freedom.'*

*And then comes the section that stirred the blood, even though the self-serving motives of many Scots nobles make it a lie:*

*'For as long as a hundred of us are left alive, we will yield in no way to English dominion. We fight not for glory nor for wealth nor honours: but only and alone we fight for freedom, which no good man surrenders but with his life.'*

# A royal dynasty
*The Normans who ruled the country*

Dundonald Castle is perhaps not as famous as Edinburgh or Stirling Castles, nonetheless it played a vital part in the history of Scotland.

For this ruin in Ayrshire acted as a springboard for some of the most momentous, not to mention tumultuous, events in Scotland's history.

This was where the Stewart line began. This dynasty of kings and pretenders, wise men and fools, spanned centuries and inevitably welded the Scots crown with that of the auld enemy, the English.

It all began in the early 12th century when King David I (*c.*1082–1153) imported noble Norman families from England in an attempt to bring some order to the often confused and bloody ways of the Scottish clans and lowland families. Among the newcomers was Walter Fitzallan, whose father had formed part of William the Conqueror's forces. Fitzallan was named as King's Steward and was given vast parcels of land in Argyll, Bute, the Lothians and Ayrshire.

It was he who built the castle at Dundonald and set about ensuring that his sons and their sons succeeded as High Steward. And as time wore on, they became known as the Stewards rather than the Fitzallans. And that eventually became Stewart.

Walter Stewart was granted the hand in marriage of Robert the Bruce's daughter Marjorie (c.1296–1316). She saw many tribulations during her short life and following a fall from a horse while pregnant, gave premature birth to a son, Robert Bruce Stewart. Sadly, Marjorie died soon after. Robert II (1316–1390) ascended to the throne in 1371, beginning a royal line that lasted for over three centuries. Dundonald, greatly improved over the years, remained his favourite home, although Robert III (c.1337–1406) moved the royal seat of power to Stirling and Edinburgh.

The first King James (1394–1437) came to the throne in 1406. There were seven in total, the most notable perhaps being James VI (1566–1625), who not only managed to live through dangerous times in his own land but also succeeded to the throne of England in 1603 upon the death of childless Elizabeth I, managing the very thing that many English kings had failed to accomplish through conquest – the union of the crowns. By that time, the spelling of the family name had changed once again, this time to Stuart, thanks to his French-influenced mother Mary, Queen of Scots (1542–1587). She had lusted after the English throne, too, but only succeeded in being imprisoned and eventually executed.

It was not all plain-sailing for the royal house of Stuart, though. James' son Charles (1600–1649) found himself at loggerheads with not only his own Parliament but also the Scottish Estates and that led to the carnage of the Civil War. His son, Charles II (1630–1685), upset the Scottish Presbyterians and that led to further revolt and more bloodshed. When his brother took the throne as James II (1633–1701) of the United Kingdom, his Roman

*Dundonald Castle, the springboard for the Stewart dynasty*

Catholic faith saw him forced to abdicate and the crown fell to his daughter Mary and her husband, William of Orange. Naturally, this caused more armed unpleasantness.

The final gasp of the Royal Stuarts came when Anne (1665–1714), Mary's sister, succeeded on the death of William. She died childless and the crown passed to her cousin, George (1660–1727), of the German House of Hanover.

As her forebear, James V, was said to have uttered as he died, 'it cam wi a lass, it'll gang wi' a lass.'

The Stewart dynasty began with Marjory and ended with Anne.

However, they continued to play an important role in UK politics. James II's son, also James (1688–1766), still laid claim to the throne and became known as The Old Pretender. His son, Charles Edward Stuart (1720–1788), ultimately led his loyal troops to disaster at Culloden, putting to the sword all hopes of a Stuart revival.

## Her end was her beginning
*The tragedy of Mary, Queen of Scots*

She is perhaps the most romantic, even controversial, Scottish monarch. Mary, Queen of Scots, (1542–1587) was the girl queen who grew to womanhood battling male dominance before suffering a premature death because of her threat to the English throne.

Mary Stewart's father, James V, was near death when she was born in Linlithgow Palace. It was on hearing the news that he had a daughter that he breathed, 'It cam wi' a lass, it'll gang wi' a lass.' The words were said to prophecy the end of the Stewart line, although Mary was not the last of the dynasty – and in fact gave birth to a son who would finally unite the crowns of Scotland.

Henry VIII saw a way to get his meaty fingers on the land to the north, by marrying her off to his infant son, the sickly Edward. When the Scots Parliament were somewhat tardy in agreeing to the match, Henry began the 'Rough Wooing', a campaign of burning and looting designed to wear down their defiance.

The child queen was spirited away to France to be cared for by the family of her mother, Mary of Guise. She helped strengthen the auld alliance by marrying the Dauphin, Francis, France's king in waiting. It was there that she began to fashion her surname as Stuart, as the letter *w* was not used in French.

She had her eyes on the English throne, claiming that she was the rightful heir to Henry's crown because Elizabeth, who had ascended to the throne in 1588, was a bastard – at least in the eyes of the Roman Catholic church. The English were not keen to oust their queen, so Mary had to make do with ruling Scotland.

By the time she returned to the land of her birth, her mother, her father-in-law King Henry II of France (1519–1559) and her young husband had all died. She arrived to face the ire of fiery Protestant leader John Knox, who did not want a Roman Catholic on the throne.

Mary was tough and cunning and knew her way around a plot. She manoeuvred and charmed and politicked through the often violent, misogynistic world of the Scottish court. In England, Elizabeth and her crafty cadre of advisors were an ever-present threat and they perhaps schemed for her to marry her second husband.

Mary met Henry Stuart, Lord Darnley, at Wemyss Castle in Fife. He was handsome, he was charming, he had royal blood – and he had a tenuous claim to the throne of England. Mary was smitten. They married but he soon showed himself to be vain, paranoid and selfish. He wanted to be king and she resisted. He conspired in the murder of her secretary, David Rizzio, because he was jealous. He had to go.

Darnley died in 1567 when an explosion ripped through the Edinburgh house in which he was staying. He had survived the blast but had then been strangled. Suspicion fell on the queen and the border freebooter James Hepburn, Earl of Bothwell. Marrying him,

*Mary, Queen of Scots*

possibly under threat, didn't help matters. It was the beginning of the end for Mary.

The nobles rebelled and demanded she renounce the crown in favour of her infant son. She fled to England to seek the protection of her cousin, Elizabeth. Amazingly, she was only 26.

That protection was a series of prisons before she was finally implicated in a plot to oust the English Queen. Her death warrant was signed, perhaps by trickery, and she was beheaded in February 1587. When the head was lifted, her red wig came free to reveal she was quite grey. And from under her dresses appeared her beloved Skye terrier to crouch beside her headless corpse.

Before her death she had embroidered on her cloth the words *In My End Is My Beginning.*

## THE BORDER BUCCANEER

*James Hepburn (1534–1578), the fourth Earl of Bothwell, was a violent, tempestuous man who fled to Norway where he was arrested as a pirate and imprisoned for ten years. When he died, his body was so disfigured by gangrene that his head was placed on the body of a dead English agent who had been sent to kill or free him. The mummified two-part corpse was placed in a coffin with a glass lid and was on display as late as 1970. However, air seeped in and ate away at the remains.*

*Bothwell's body was finally encased in a wooden coffin, and placed in the church crypt.*

## THE LAST KING OF SCOTLAND

*Mary's son, James VI (1566– 1625), was a scholar and author dubbed 'The Wisest Fool in Christendom'. He was responsible for sponsoring the translation of the Bible that is still used today – the King James Edition.*

*He was also extremely paranoid – and with good reason. During his lifetime there were a number of threats against his life, not the least being the notorious Gunpowder Plot.*

*He also disliked smoking and called it 'a custom loathsome to the eye, hateful to the nose…' in his work* A Counterblaste to Tobacco *(1604).*

*His belief in the divine right of kings, inherited by his son and grandson, did not sit well with his Parliament and ultimately led to the civil wars.*

# THE MONSTROUS REGIMENT OF WOMEN

For centuries, history was a man's game, with the contributions of women ignored, sidelined or even air-brushed out of the annals. There are certain notable exceptions, like Mary, Queen of Scots, who are difficult to write off completely. It was Mary's great nemesis, that vicious, bitter old misogynistic result of his times, John Knox, who published a treatise against female rule, which he called The First Blast of the Trumpet Against the Monstrous Regiment of Women.

Here are a few women who have contributed in some way to history, art and culture.

## Crowning achievement
*The woman who defied convention to support a king*

When Robert the Bruce had himself crowned at Scone in 1306, the ceremony was not performed according to tradition, which dictated that it be carried out by a member of the Clan MacDuff. That was why there was a second ceremony the following day – and the person who placed the crown on his head was a woman.

Isabella MacDuff, Countess of Buchan (possibly 1270–1314) was a formidable character. Her husband sided with the English during the Wars of Independence – he was a Comyn and naturally did not take kindly to the Bruce killing his cousin in Dumfries. However, Isabella turned against him and sided with the Scots. She missed the first crowning at Scone but when the Bruce agreed to replay the whole thing, she was the person who officially anointed him King. He would not have been seated on the Stone of Destiny, as tradition dictated, as Edward I had already

stolen it away.

Naturally, this did not endear her to the English king. With the early wars not going well for Scotland, Isabella found herself a captive, thanks to betrayal by a Scottish noble, and sent to Berwick. There she was to be put on display as a warning to others.

Isabella was held in a wood and iron cage which dangled from the walls of Berwick Castle or was in such a position as to be in full view of the populace. The Bruce's sister, Mary, suffered similar humiliation at Roxburgh Castle. The Scottish King's other sister, Christian, was sent to a nunnery while his wife was held in virtual solitary

confinement in a manor house.

Isabella was kept in that cage for four years before she, too, was sent to a convent to be held as a hostage against future negotiations with the Scots.

### 'BLACK' AGNES'S LOVE ARROWS

*Agnes Randolph, Countess of Dunbar (1300–1360) was said to have been as determined as she was beautiful. Her stunning shock of black hair gave her the nickname 'Black Agnes'.*

*In 1337 she was at home in Dunbar Castle when the English laid siege. She took command of the defensive forces with such skill that she held the much larger army outside the walls at bay for six months. When the English war*

*The remains of Dunbar Castle*

*machines bombarded the walls, she had maids flick away the dust from the battlements. When an arrow hit the man standing beside the English commander, he remarked, 'Agnes's love arrows pierce the heart.'*

*Finally, the siege was lifted and the English left, stung they had been stymied by a mere woman.*

## THE HONOURS OF SCOTLAND

*The crown Isabella placed on Bruce's head is said to now form part of the oldest Royal Regalia in Britain, known as the Honours of Scotland.*

*These are the Crown, Sceptre and Sword of State which were first used in their current condition at the coronation of Mary, Queen of Scots in 1543.*

*The Honours are housed in Edinburgh Castle along with the Stone of Scone, the Stone of Destiny, on which Scottish Kings sat as the crown was placed on their head. It had been taken by Edward I and was housed in Westminster until it was returned home in 1996.*

## THE TRAGIC PRINCESS

*Marjorie Bruce (1297–1316) was the eldest daughter of Robert the Bruce, to his first wife who died soon after the child was born – ironically the same age as her daughter when she died. She was around nine when she was captured by Scots forces loyal to the English and was originally to be displayed in a cage at the Tower of London but was instead confined in a convent.*

*When finally released, she was promised in marriage to Walter Stewart. In March, 1316, she fell from her horse while heavily pregnant. Her son, destined to be Robert II, was born prematurely in nearby Paisley Abbey but Marjorie died within hours.*

# Courage and fidelity
*The gentle presence who
saved a Prince*

The role of Fionnghal nic Dhòmhnaill, or Flora MacDonald (1722–1790), in the escape of Bonnie Prince Charlie is well-known.

Despite her father and her fiancée being loyal to the Crown, she helped the Prince flee in a bonny boat over the sea to Skye and then to the island of Raasay.

But what happened to her after the Prince got into drag to pretend to be her maid servant?

When captured, 24-year-old Flora was imprisoned for a time in Dunstaffnage Castle in Oban and the Tower of London but was released to return to Scotland. She married Allan MacDonald and such was her fame she met with English writer, wit and cultural commentator Samuel Johnson when he and James Boswell visited the Western Isles in 1773. He described her as 'a woman of middle stature, soft features, elegant manners and gentle presence.'

*Flora MacDonald, who helped save a prince*

However, in 1774, with debts rising, Flora and her husband left Scotland for the Americas, settling in North Carolina.

Scotland's notions of rebellion may have been snuffed out but the scent of freedom was fresh in the colonies. Despite her aid to the Jacobite cause as a young woman, Flora and her husband were loyal to the British and during the revolutionary wars she found herself a prisoner again, this time of the American militia. Allan had been taken in battle and was a prisoner of war.

With her plantation destroyed and life in the Americas no longer appealing, she decided to return to Scotland in 1779 but her adventures were not yet complete. During an attack on her ship by French privateers, she refused to take refuge below decks and was wounded on the arm.

She died on Skye in 1790 and was buried wrapped in a sheet said to have been used by Charles Edward Stuart. Her tombstone tells the world she was the 'Preserver of Prince Charles Edward Stuart'. It also carries the words of Dr Samuel Johnson:

*'Her name will be mentioned in history and if courage and fidelity be virtues, mentioned with honour.'*

## A TASTE OF SCOTLAND

*Bonnie Prince Charlie gave Flora MacDonald a locket containing his portrait as they parted on the isle of Raasay.*

*That wasn't the only thing he was said to have left on the islands. The Prince was very fond of a dram – too fond perhaps in his later years – and tradition states that, as a thank you to those who aided him on Skye, he left the secret of his favourite tipple, which was said to have been created for him by Royal Apothecaries.*

*That drink became known as Drambuie, from* **an dram buidheach**, *the drink that satisfies.*

# The woman with star power
*The top science writer who educated herself*

At a time when reading was considered 'unladylike', Mary Somerville (1780–1872) not only managed to educate herself but also rose to become one of the world's top science writers.

Born in Jedburgh in the Borders, the daughter of a naval officer named Fairfax, Mary found herself restricted by the views of her day that women should be seen and not learned. She was given a rudimentary education at boarding school but took to reading everything she could in order to further her knowledge. She was supported in this by her uncle, Thomas Somerville.

She continued her studies in science and mathematics during a short-lived marriage to a cousin, Captain Samuel Greig, an officer in the Russian Navy, even though he had a poor opinion of the intellectual abilities of her gender. His death in 1807 left her free to pursue her learning curve and also to marry, in 1812, naval surgeon William Somerville, another cousin who was far more supportive of her efforts.

Taking up residence in London, she began to move in more liberal circles, meeting many top minds of the day – including astronomers, scientists, physicists and mathematicians. In 1826 she published her first paper, *'On the Magnetizing Power of the More Refrangible Solar Rays.'*

A condensed version of a book on celestial mechanics was

*Mathematician Mary Somerville*

acclaimed and she and Caroline Herschel, a German astronomer noted for finding several comets, became the first women to be given honorary membership of the Royal Astronomical Society.

In 1836, Somerville suggested the existence of an unknown planet, which led to the discovery of Neptune by astronomer John Couch Adams.

Her work and achievement saw her being awarded a pension of £200 a year, on the recommendation of Prime Minister Sir Robert Peel.

She continued her work in mathematics and the sciences, published more books, including one when she was 89 years old. Even when she lost her hearing and her health began to fail, she was reading and solving problems. She died in Italy at the age of 92. Seven years later Somerville College was founded in Oxford, which initially admitted only women.

## VOTE RIGGING HITS WRONG NOTE

*In 2017, Mary Somerville became the first non-royal woman to appear on a Royal Bank of Scotland banknote.*

*The face to appear on the ten pound note had been put to a public vote and she was the clear front runner ahead of Thomas Telford and physicist James Clerk Maxwell, a hero of Albert Einstein.*

*However, a last minute surge of votes, many from abroad, seemed to put Telford in front but the voting pattern was deemed dodgy – automated systems may have been used – so the bank decided to stick with Somerville, who they believed was the clear public choice.*

## Queen of the Comstock
*From Fife to the wilds of Nevada*

Alison Orum (1826–1903) was born in Forfar but led a life of excitement, tribulation and danger in the American West – and built one of the most impressive mansions in the territory.

She and her husband, Stephen Hunter, emigrated to the USA when she was still a teenager and he converted to Mormonism. The marriage lasted only a few years before they parted and eventually she married again, to Alexander Cowan, and found herself living on the frontier of Utah Territory. That marriage failed, too, and she opened a boarding house in Nevada, then enjoying the gold rush sparked by the discovery of the Comstock Load.

Her crude lodging house made her a living, which she supplemented by telling fortunes with a crystal ball she brought with her from Scotland and taking in washing. However, she struck it rich when she came into possession of shares in mining claims.

She married again, to muleskinner, or muleteer, Lemuel Sandford Bowers and when their claims were merged into one, they proved to be very rich in silver.

Soon Eilley Bowers, as she was now known, was one of the wealthiest women in the territory and she showed it off. She built a fabulous $300,000 mansion in the middle of the silver fields, which boasted marble fireplaces, chandeliers and a fountain. Other millionaire prospectors had impressive homes but the Bowers Mansion was one of the most expensive houses ever constructed on the frontier. She styled herself the Queen of the Comstock and on a trip to Europe she believed she was entitled to an audience with Queen Victoria. When that was refused she clipped a piece of ivy from the wall of Westminster Abbey, which she planted on her return to Comstock. She told friends it was a gift from the Queen.

She also returned with a baby daughter, named Margaret Persia. Eilley never explained where the child came from.

*The Bowers mansion*

When the silver played out, the Bowers faced hard times and when her husband died in 1868, at the age of 35, Eilley opened the mansion as a resort to stave off debts. However, she eventually had to sell up and move on, leaving not just her husband's grave but also her daughter's, who died in 1874.

Eilley died penniless in Oakland, California. The Bowers Mansion still stands and is administered by the Parks Department.

# Fighting the pestilence of the free winds
*The free thinker who battled slavery*

Frances, or Fanny, Wright (1795–1852) was of Scottish birth but became an ardent abolitionist and feminist in America in the days it was dangerous to be so liberal minded.

Born in Dundee, she inherited her parents' fortune when she was only three and was brought up in London by relatives. It was one of them, progressive thinker James Milne, who encouraged the young Frances to think for herself and to question accepted rules and conventions.

She educated herself and wrote her first book by the age of 18. She arrived in New York in 1818 to produce a play she had written about Swiss Independence. More books followed, including one in which she praised American democracy.

It was during another visit to the United States, in the company of French soldier the Marquis de

Lafayette, who was being honoured as a hero of the Revolutionary Wars, that she took up the cause of abolitionism. 'The sight of slavery is revolting everywhere,' she wrote. 'But to inhale the impure breath of its pestilence in the free winds of America is odious beyond all that imagination can conceive.'

At New Harmony, on the Wabash River in South Indiana, she met Welsh reformer Robert Owen, a mill owner known to Scotland for his good works in New Lanark. His idea was to establish a utopian society in the USA but it failed after a few years.

Frances Wright decided to set up her own colony, the Nashoba Commune, in which slaves, bought from their white owners, could work for themselves. She laboured to make it a success, helping to clear the land herself, but ultimately the experiment failed. The men and women she had hoped to set off on a new life were taken by her to the slavery-free Republic of Haiti where they could live as free people as long as they worked hard.

Frances Wright continued to fight for abolition, for women's rights, education and birth control. She also became notorious for her scandalous personal life, earning her the title 'The Great Red Harlot'. She married disastrously and ended her days fighting her husband for control of what money she had left. She died, aged 57, following a fall on ice in Cincinnati, Ohio, where she was buried.

*Abolitionist and free-thinker, Frances Wright*

## IMPROVING THE LAND

*In 1852 one book helped promote the cause of abolition. Harriet Beecher Stowe's* **Uncle Tom's Cabin** *is not as well thought of today but it was one of the most popular novels of its century.*

*The author was not so inspired to right a wrong when she visited the highlands of Scotland and was shown the results of the 'improvements' by the Duke and Duchess of Sutherland in clearing the land of its people to make way for sheep farms and increasing their wealth. She wrote that the often brutal clearances were 'an almost sublime instance of the benevolent employment of superior wealth...'*

# Woman with a mission
*The African adventures of Mary Slessor*

David Livingston is perhaps better known but the achievements of Mary Slessor (1848–1915) were no less inspiring.

It was Livingston's exploits that planted the desire to take up missionary work in Africa. However, Aberdeen – born Mary was a mere worker in the Dundee jute mills, supporting her family since the death of her alcoholic father. She was self-educated and without the patronage of well-off Christians but that did not prevent her from applying to work with the Church of Scotland foreign missions and in 1876 was on her way to the Calabar Coast in southern Nigeria

Mary, thanks to her humble upbringing, was no delicate flower. She cut her red hair short and dressed in trousers, much to the dismay of some fellow missionaries, to stride through the bush and jungle with confidence, carrying her own load. At first she was a typical western missionary, seeing the people there as mere heathens. But she changed. She learned the language. She fought injustice. She lived with the people, and, unlike other missionaries, ate their food. She came through tropical disease, faced armed natives and saved hundreds of twin babies, believed by their tribe to be the spawn of evil. Mary took the children in at the mission, adopting one, Janie, as her own daughter. She became the British Empire's first ever female magistrate and was hailed as the White Queen of Okoyong, after one of the tribes with which she worked.

Her health, and family issues, meant she had to return often to Scotland but she was always drawn back to Africa.

She died at her mission, her body unable to fight one more fever attack. She remains honoured in Calabar, while in 1997 her image appeared on the Clydesdale Bank's ten pound note. In 2015, the centenary of her death, an asteroid belt was named after her.

## A QUEEN'S FAVOURITE
*She was compared with Jane Austen, was said to be Queen Victoria's favourite writer and yet, despite having written nearly 200 novels and short stories, Mrs Oliphant (1828–1897) is relatively unknown today.*

*Born in Edinburgh but raised in Glasgow and Liverpool, Margaret Oliphant published her first book –* **Passages in the life of Margaret Maitland of Sunnyside** *– in 1849 and kept on writing.*

*Author Margaret Oliphant*

*She married in 1857 but her husband died seven years later of tuberculosis and to feed herself, her three children, and also her extended family, she stepped up productivity. She produced domestic dramas, historical novels, supernatural tales and attacks on social injustice in relation to the treatment of women. She knew sadness well. In addition to her husband, she saw her daughter Maggie die in 1864 and then her two sons, Cyril and Francis in 1894.*

# FOOD AND DRINK

A feast of tasty facts about the Scottish diet.

## The Selkirk Grace
*Robert Burns gave a traditional prayer international appeal*

Some hae meat and canna eat,
And some would eat that want it;
But we hae meat, and we can eat,
Sae let the Lord be thankit.

The Selkirk Grace was said to have been created off the cuff by Robert

*Robert Burns*

Burns at a dinner held by the Earl of Selkirk. However, a version of it was known in Galloway prior to the poet putting quill to parchment as the Galloway Grace or the Covenanter's Grace.

It is still used to begin the festivities at Burns Suppers.

## The Water of Life
*The moonshiners who battled to save their national drink*

Scottish author and poet Tobias Smollett (1721–1771) noted in his final novel *Humphrey Clinker* that Lowlanders liked to drink a 'thin, yeasty beverage, made of malt' called pippany. He said it tasted very like English table beer. However, the people of the north had a nectar of their very own:

'The Highlanders, on the contrary, despise this liquor, and regale themselves with whisky, a malt spirit as strong as geneva (gin), which they swallow in great quantities, without any signs of inebriation: They are used to it from the cradle, and find it an excellent preservative against the winter cold, which must be extreme on these mountains – I am told it is given with great success to infants, as cordial, in the confluent smallpox, when the eruption seems to flag, and the symptoms grow unfavourable.'

Not for nothing, then, is whisky called *Uisge Beatha*, the water of life.

It may have been brought to Scotland from Ireland, but then the art of distilling malt and barley might have been taken there by St Patrick, who could have been a Scot.

The earliest record of the spirit is in 1495 when the Exchequer Rolls of Scotland record that eight bolls of malt were given to Friar John Coll by the king to make *aquae vitae* (Latin for 'Water of Life').

That quantity of malt would have produced around 1,500 bottles of the spirit which was taken, as Smollett noted, often for its medicinal properties. The fact that a Friar was named is also noteworthy, for it was monks, driven from their abbeys during the Reformation, who helped spread the distillation skills and tended to the sick.

Distilling the spirit was so popular – it was said that no self-respecting laird would buy their dram, for they had their own stills – that by the 17th century the government realised there was a revenue stream they were overlooking.

Increased taxes, combined with the desire by the authorities to tame the often rambunctious clans, helped force the local stills underground.

Robert Burns, who was fond of a tincture now and then, immortalised the memory of the 'Ferintosh', distilled by Forbes of Culloden, which was declared illegal after Bonnie Prince Charlie's failed rising.

*'Thee Ferintosh! oh, sadly lost,*
*Scotland lament frae coast to coast;*
*Now colic grips and barkin' hoast*
*May kill us 'aw,*
*For loyal Forbes's charter boast*
*Is ta'en awa.'*

The poet, himself an exciseman for a time, then goes on to damn 'thae curst leeches o' the Excise.'

Illicit stills became a growth industry in the 17th and 18th centuries. They sprang up in the glens and hills, on the islands, even in cities – at one point Edinburgh had 400 stills buried in cellars or underground, anywhere there could be a makeshift chimney to dispel the smoke.

It was that smoke that was often the dead giveaway and drew the attention of the excisemen, the gaugers as they were known. However, the smugglers worked out ways to signal to one another that the law was about to descend.

By the 1820s, despite the revenue men seizing 14,000 stills a year, the flow of illegal whisky was unstemmed. An Act was passed in 1825 that allowed a distillery to operate at a fee of £10 for a forty gallon still. The first to be granted was to George Smith of Glenlivet. Sixty years later, the High Court decreed that only the liquor from his distillery could be called Glenlivet.

It didn't completely stamp out the potstill trade but it did lay the groundwork for an industry which is now one of the country's most important and iconic industries. Whisky is exported to more than 200 countries and generates around £4 billion a year for the economy.

## FIELD OF BLOOD

*The Campsie Hills, which lie between Glasgow and the wild north, was a popular area for the production of tax-free whisky. One day, a band of McGregors in the process of lifting cattle found an illicit still. Unfortunately for them, it did not prove to be the water of life because the owners of the cattle they had stolen waited until they had drunk themselves senseless, then killed the lot. Not surprisingly, the location of the*

*slaughter became known as the Field of Blood.*

## THE OTHER AMBER NECTAR

*They say it is Scotland's other national drink, after whisky. They say it's made from girders. It has regularly knocked other products into second place in the thirsts of fizzy-drink loving Scots.*

*Irn-Bru is a rust-coloured, tangy, carbonated drink made to a secret recipe known only to three people, two members of the Barr family and a company board member whose identity is kept confidential.*

*It is known that it contains small amounts of the food additive ammonium ferric citrate, hence the Irn.*

*And it has its own tartan, orange and blue in colour, accredited in 1997 by the Council of the Scottish Tartans Society.*

# Great Chieftan o' the pudding race
*Making a meal of offal*

There is no more traditionally Scottish fayre than the haggis. Or, at least, you'd think so.

Robert Burns composed an address to it, naming it the 'great chieftan o' the pudding race', and the haggis was even mentioned by an earlier poet, William Dunbar (1416–1513), in *The Flyting of Dunbar and Kennedy*.

However, its origins may not have been in Scotland. There are references to something similar in Homer's Odyssey, while the Romans were known to make such a dish. The Vikings can also lay claim to their version and all – except perhaps the ancient Greeks – could have brought it to our shores.

Even England, the 'auld enemy', lays claim to a pudding called *haggus*, or *haggas*.

The Scots have a love/hate relationship with the dish but do delight in telling foreigners that the haggis is a strange, three-legged creature that roams wild among the heather. One of the legs is shorter than the other to help it flee the hunters along the hillside.

The fact is, haggis is a poor man's meal. It is made from offal – essentially the hard-to-cook sheep's pluck (liver, heart and lungs, the latter also known as the lights) mixed with beef suet, onions, oatmeal and salt and black pepper for seasoning.

The casing of the haggis is the large bag that is sheep's stomach, or the 'king's hood', a smaller stomach bag. Both have to be properly cleaned, of course, and soaked in cold, salted water for 12 hours. The 'pluck' is then boiled with the animal's windpipe, still attached, hanging over the side of the pot to allow the impurities to be expelled. Only half of the liver is used and it, like the heart and lungs, is minced

up and placed in the bag.

The old Scots word *hag* means to chop or hew and that may be how the dish earned its name, although the Swedish word *hogga* also has a similar meaning. It should also be noted that the French word for chopping is *hacher*.

The whole thing is then boiled, the bag being pricked to prevent swelling and bursting.

Traditionally it is served with neeps (turnips) and tatties (potatoes). Naturally, you should also have a wee nip of whisky, too – detractors say this is to kill the taste of the food. Haggis can, however, be fried and used as a breakfast food, but generally without the whisky.

Nowadays, though, the casing is synthetic and the entire dish is purchased ready mixed.

The Romans were said to have used a pig's stomach for the bag and included brains in the mixture, as well as raw eggs and pulped pineapples. There was also a concoction made up of the putrefied intestines of fish mixed with wine and spices.

Pork, however, was not a staple of the Scots diet while pineapples were hard to come by in the mountains and glens of northern Britain. It's worth noting that the Cajuns use a stuffed pork stomach in a dish called 'paunce'.

Real Scottish haggis has been unknown in the USA, thanks to a 1971 ban on foods containing sheep's lung. American Burns' Suppers have to make-do with specially made lung-free haggis or a vegetarian version.

## THE IMMORTAL MEMORY

*Haggis and whisky play a central role in celebrations of the life of Scotland's National Poet, Robert Burns (1759–1796).*

*At Burns Night events, on or near 25 January each year, the Haggis is delivered with great solemnity, led by a piper, before a nominated guest recites the poet's* **Address to the Haggis.** *The pudding is then sliced with some ceremony, perhaps with a dirk, and dished out around the room.*

*Naturally, although not mandatory, whisky is consumed.*

*There then follows an evening of recitation, conviviality and, of course, more whisky.*

---

## SUPER TONIC

*If it wasn't for Edinburgh-born army doctor George Cleghorn, millions around the world might not enjoy a gin and tonic.*

*Around 1736, he discovered that quinine could combat malaria, so it was added to water laced with sugar and soda. However, the taste of this 'tonic water' was so dreadful that officers of the British East India Company added some of their gin ration to it, as well as some lime – and the G&T was born!*

# Squared away
*The mystery of Scotland's favourite sausage*

Scotland is a country of hills and mountains. Only the sausage is flat.

Why Scottish sausage is the shape it is – call it square, sliced, square sliced, simply flat or even round – puzzles visitors who are more used to their morning meat being, well, sausage-shaped and squeezed into a casing.

The square sausage is traditionally made of beef, not pork. Scots are very fond of their beef, as the heart disease statistics will testify.

Despite the ubiquity of the flat sausage, Scots are not nationalistic when it comes to their food and will eat 'links', as the more traditional sausage-shaped breakfast meats are known. Their home-grown version, though, is far easier to cook thanks to its frying pan or grill-friendly shape.

Exactly when the first square sausage appeared is not known. It is widely accepted that it was at some point in the late 19th century, when tins were being produced cheaply and someone came up with the genius notion that a squarish tin could be used to make the sausages without the annoyance – and expense – of squeezing the meat in a skin. Beef was also more readily available, thanks to cheaper imports.

The name given to the better sausage is Lorne. Why is open to conjecture.

The most common explanation is that the Glasgow comedian Tommy Lorne gave his name to the foodstuff due to his fondness for them and his habit of making jokes about them. One of his catchphrases was 'Sausages are the boys.'

However, there are newspaper advertisements using the name Lorne Sausage from before he ever took to the stage. Given his real name was Hugh Corcoran, it's far more likely that he, in fact, took his stage name from the sausage.

There is a theory that the food was named after the ancient district of Lorne, now part of Argyll and Bute on the West of Scotland. Perhaps the very first square sausage was made there.

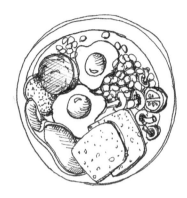

*Square sausage forms the centrepiece of the 'full Scottish breakfast'*

Or perhaps it was named after the local laird, the Marquess of Lorne (better known as the Duke of Argyll).

The naming of foods after famous people was common. The sandwich, for instance, was named for the Earl of Sandwich, who was reputed to have invented it by slapping some meat between two slices of bread during a long session of gaming. The Garibaldi biscuit was named after the famed Italian general. The Peach Melba after singer Nelly Melba.

In 2009, there was a call to have

the Lorne Sausage given protected status, like the Arbroath Smokie (a distinctive kipper), so that only sausages made in Scotland could use the name.

When visiting Scotland always ensure that you are offered a proper Lorne Sausage, preferably Steak Lorne. There are cheaper products which do not bear the name Lorne and are comprised of 'mystery meat' and bulked up with fat which vanishes on frying, leaving you with a pitiful, shrivelled chunk of something tasteless.

The Lorne sausage can be eaten as part of the full Scottish breakfast, or wedged into a breakfast roll. Ketchup or brown sauce can be added as per the diner's tastes. If you want the experience of a limited full Scottish while on the fly, a fried egg and even a potato scone can be added to the roll.

However, not everyone is as enamoured of the Lorne as the Scots. In a Japanese guidebook published in 2012, it was advised that the sausage is best avoided.

Ah well, you can't please everyone. True Scots avoid raw fish.

## THE GLASGOW CURRY

*Glaswegians lay claim to the creation of one of the nation's favourite curries – the Chicken Tikka Masala.*

*There is no doubt that the origins of the dish lie in India – the word tikka means pieces or small bits – but one chef insisted that he was the one who came up with the current fusion of chicken, sauce and spices.*

*Ali Ahmed Aslam, owner of the Shish Mahal restaurant, claimed that he responded to a customer's request for more sauce in his curry by adding spices soaked in condensed tomato soup.*

*Similar claims are made in other cities but never argue with a Glaswegian.*

## Ale that was sweeter than honey
*The legend of Heather Ale*

The denizens above Hadrian's Wall may not have invented beer but they may have developed their own distinct brew. Until comparatively recently, the existence of an ale made from 'heather bells' was hidden by legend, the recipe thought long dead.

The drinking of it brought glory, strength and courage, while one chronicler, much later, said that it was 'one of the pleasures which the souls of departed heroes enjoyed in the society of the gods.' (WT Marchant, 1888). Although

it'd be interesting to see what the Advertising Standards Authority would have to say about that.

Robert Louis Stevenson once wrote:

*From the bonny bells of heather,*
*They brewed a drink lang syne,*
*Was sweeter far than honey,*
*Was stronger far than wine.*

The legend of Heather Ale goes back to the time of the Picts. Highlanders, it is said, enjoyed a drink made from heather, honey and sugar even into the early 20th century but the Pictish tipple needed no additional ingredients. However, the recipe was a closely guarded secret. Anyone who tasted the nectar wanted to know how to make it but the Picts remained close-mouthed.

The legend goes that when the Scots and the Picts clashed and the Scots were triumphant, after a great deal of slaughter and general unpleasantness, only two men remained who knew the trick of manufacture, a father and son. (Another version has it as the king and his son, yet another that it was a man, a brother and his son. That's the thing about legends – they're like Scottish hills. Always another one up ahead).

An ultimatum was delivered – cough up the recipe or be tortured and killed. The man had lost everything but was determined that the secret would not be lost to the invaders. However, he struck a bargain – if the Scots would kill his son, he would tell them.

The Scots did so – depending on which version of the tale you prefer, he was either cracked over the head in front of his father or thrown from the cliffs at the Mull of Galloway.

With his son dead, the man was satisfied that he could prevent the Scots from ever learning the true way of fermenting Heather Ale and he refused to tell them anything. A deal may be a deal, but a good drink is something to protect. The Scots followed through on their threat and killed him. Or, he took his own life by throwing himself from the cliff, too.

Whatever happened, the secret of the Pictish Heather Ale died with him.

However, in recent years it has been revived. In 2011, a batch based on a Neolithic recipe was brewed in Milwaukee, Wisconsin, as part of an Ale Through the Ages brewing seminar. They built their recipe on archaeological data and pollen fragments found in pottery unearthed at various sites in Scotland.

Now the *Leann Fraoich* (Gaelic for Heather Ale) has been revived by Scottish brewers Williams Brothers and, it is claimed, may be the oldest style of beer in the world. Their brew sees flowering heather and sweet gale – or bogmyrtle – mixed with the malted barley. Later, the liquid is tipped into a vat of more heather flowers and left to ferment.

Whether any of these are the same drink brewed by the Picts, who were said to have used no additives, is open to question.

## THE JOKE FOOD THAT CROSSED THE GLOBE

*Only a Scot would think of dipping a popular chocolate bar in batter, deep frying it and serving with ice cream, or even chips.*

*The Carron Fish Bar, previously The Haven, in Stonehaven on the Aberdeenshire coast has claimed to be ground zero for the deep fried Mars bar. A Scottish daily newspaper then spread the word.*

*As the news crossed the globe, it became something of a joke, not to mention sneering, about the notoriously poor diet of Scots but a number of enterprising chip shop owners added it to their menu.*

*It is worth noting that the manufacturers do not endorse the process as is does not promote a healthy and active lifestyle.*

## OAT CUISINE

*The highland village of Carrbridge has played host to the World Porridge Making Championships since 1996. Contenders come from all over the world to the village hall in the Cairngorms to compete for the title and go home with the Gold Spurtle trophy.*

*A spurtle is a baton-shaped wooden stirring implement that is vital in the preparation of real porridge.*

*The competition has seen some unique embellishments to the traditional dish, including fried eggs, sticky toffee and chorizo.*

# SCOTLAND AT WAR

Scottish history has been described as 'one long brawl' and it is not far from the truth. When Scots weren't fighting Romans or the English, they were battling among themselves for land, for honour, or just for the sheer hell of it.

## The lost legion
*What happened to the men of the ninth?*

In 117 AD, the Ninth Legion of the Roman Army marched from their base in York and into the mists of Scotland. They left a mystery that has exercised the minds of authors and filmmakers, particularly Rosemary Sissons whose 1954 novel *The Eagle of the Ninth* brought the story into the public consciousness.

For the force of warriors, toughened in battle and veterans of Rome's furthest outpost, seemed to completely disappear.

Whatever happened, it eventually resulted in the creation of a dividing line across the island that exists to this day.

The legion, raised in Spain, was one of the premier units of the Roman army and had been part of the invasion force in 43 AD. It was a relatively easy conquest and southern England seemed happy to become part of the Empire. Things were not so easy in Northern England, Wales and Scotland.

When Boudicca raised the Iceni tribe against the Roman overlords in 61 AD, the men of the Ninth were in the thick of it and suffered huge losses. When their numbers were replenished they came down hard on the local people.

The legion helped build York, where they based themselves. There was sporadic trouble with the local tribe, the *Brigantes*, but the real problem lay to the north, in the rough lands of Caledonia, where the Painted People, the *Picti*, lived.

And it was against them that the men of the Ninth marched on that day in 117 AD.

No one knows for certain what happened, for of the fate of the Ninth nothing is recorded.

They say there was a dreadful battle during which the Picts wreaked revenge for the slaughter at Mons Graupius over 30 years earlier. They say that the men were picked off one-by-one in the mist-shrouded mountains of the north, for the Roman Army had trouble coping with guerrilla warfare.

None of the above was the case, say academics. The men of the Ninth were simply transferred and may have been involved in wars elsewhere. But there is little evidence of that.

What is known is that more men were rushed into Britain. The garrison at York had to be reinforced. The Emperor Hadrian was so concerned with the situation in the far province that he ordered the building of the wall that bears his name to keep the savage tribes at bay.

The border between what would become Scotland and England had been established.

*A crack Roman legion vanished without trace in Scotland*

---

### THE FIRST BATTLE

*The first Scot to properly step into history was a warrior called Calgacus, or Calgaich. He was the leader of the northern tribe the Romans called the Caledonii. They were tall and muscular and red-haired and it was they, one summer's day in 84 AD, who faced the invading Roman army on a hill dubbed as Mons Graupius by the historian Tacitus. It was he who gave Calgacus – the Swordsman – his speech of defiance, saying that the Romans 'make a desert and they call it peace.'*

*The Romans faced 30,000 tribesmen that day and slaughtered a third. The survivors, including Calgacus, melted into the hills and valleys, but were not pursued with any great vigour by the Romans, who pulled back beyond the Tay.*

*The blood and thunder of Scottish history had begun.*

## THE MISPRINT THAT NAMED A MOUNTAIN RANGE

*No one is certain exactly where the battle of Mons Graupius was fought. More than a dozen sites have been put forward, all in the north-east of Scotland.*

*It was a mis-print in a 16th century printed copy of a biography of the Roman general Julius Agricola by Tacitus that gave the mountain range in the area its name. Instead of Graupius, the printer set Grampius – and the Grampians were born.*

# The deaths that caused a crisis
*An Auld Alliance is struck*

A king's desire to be with his new wife was the cause of the bloody Wars of Independence.

Alexander III (1249–1286) was in such a rush to reach his bride Yolande that he fell from his horse on the cliffs at Kinghorn in Fife and broke his neck.

The crown fell to his grand-daughter, four-year-old Margaret, the Maid of Norway, and Edward I of England, the dead king's brother-in-law, saw the chance to properly establish his claim that he, in fact, ruled Scotland by marrying her off to his son. However, little Margaret died on the way to Scotland.

The Scottish crown lay fallow and thirteen different competitors claimed the right to rule, including John Balliol and Robert Bruce (the later king's grandfather). Edward was invited to decide who had the more valid claim and he settled on Balliol.

It became clear that Edward saw the new King of Scots as little more than his puppet. His demand that an

*The spot where Alexander died at Kinghorn*

## THEY KNEEL BEFORE ME...

*The breacbannoch was a reliquary said to have contained the bones of either St Columba or St Andrew – and according to legend it was brought onto the field at Bannockburn to allow the Scots army to pray to it. When he saw the opposition kneeling, Edward thought that they were begging him for mercy but he was soon disabused of that notion.*

*The breacbannoch is now lost, although there was a school of thought that it was the Monymusk Reliquary. This wooden and leather casket with silver and copper adornments is now held by the Museum of Scotland but whatever relics it once held have been long lost from history.*

army be raised to fight for England led to the Scots striking a treaty with Edward's other enemy, France. Thus was born the Auld Alliance between the two countries that they would come to each other's aid when threatened by England.

Edward marched north to bring the Scots to heel – and the wars had begun. Balliol was captured and in a humiliating display, the arms of his country were ripped from his tunic. From then on, he was known as 'Toom Tabard' – the empty coat.

# Death of a king
*The flowers of the forest are cut down*

For a time in the early 16th century there was peace between Scotland and England. The king, James IV (1473–1513) wasn't perfect but he was loved and he had married Margaret Tudor, the daughter of Henry VII. However, when Henry VIII took to the throne, the situation changed and soon the two countries were drawing swords and priming cannon.

It came to a head in September 1513 at Flodden, near Norham in Northumberland when James himself led his army into battle. It was a bloody affair, with one survivor saying that the men cut and slashed at each other until it became so dark they couldn't see who they were fighting and the mud under their feet had turned blood-red.

It was a disaster for the Scottish army and society in general. Ten thousand Scots perished on that rain-soaked battlefield, including the king. Around him lay the bodies of much of his nobility, immortalised in verse and song as the Flowers of the Forest.

> *The Flooers o' the Forest, that fought aye the foremost,*
> *The pride o' oor land lie cauld in the clay.*
> *(Jean Elliot, 1756)*

*The border town of Selkirk lost many men at Flodden*

James IV's body was found on the field and taken first to Berwick, where it was embalmed, and then sent in a lead coffin to London. His bloody coat was sent to Henry, then fighting in France, as a trophy. The body was stored away in a Surrey monastery until Elizabethan workman found it, cut off the head and used it as a football. A nobleman finally took possession of the head and placed it on display in his home until it was finally buried in an anonymous grave.

In Edinburgh, fear that the English would invade prompted the building of the Flodden Wall, parts of which can still be seen near the Grassmarket and in historic Greyfriars Kirkyard.

### THE KING KILLED BY A LION

*James II (1437–1460), known as 'the fiery face' due to a livid birthmark, had a great love of artillery – and it proved his undoing.*

*He found himself on the Lancastrian side in the Wars of the Roses and was attempting to wrest Roxburgh Castle from English control. As he stood by it, a great cannon called The Lion exploded and killed him.*

# The Not-So-English Civil War
*The wars of the three crowns*

There is a tendency to term the Cavaliers-v-Roundheads unpleasantness of 1642–1651 the English Civil Wars but that is a blatant misnomer.

There is a case to be made that if it weren't for events in Scotland and Ireland, there may not have been a war at all.

Hostilities could be said to have been begun by Scottish forces. This was prompted by religious differences – Charles I wanted to introduce Episcopalianism and the staunch Scottish Presbyterians were having none of it. Relations deteriorated, there was some minor fighting, and then in 1640 the Scots sallied forth into England with a force of 20,000-plus infantry and cavalry. A lacklustre and inferior force sent by the King was defeated at Newbury-on-Tyne and in order to avoid the ignominious fate of losing the north of England to Scotland, Charles not only agreed to the Scottish demands but also coughed up £200,000.

When Cromwell's forces rebelled in England, both sides pitched woo at the Scots but it was the Parliamentary side who were deemed the more acceptable

*The monument to the Battle of Dunbar*

suitor, thanks to promises (never kept) that Presbyterianism would rule supreme across the land. The Scots army fell in line with Cromwell and fought with him at Marston Moor in July 1644.

Meanwhile, back in Scotland, the Royalist Marquis of Montrose (1612–1650) was proving to be troublesome. He had linked up with an Irish force and during what became known as the Year of Miracles fought his way through every army and impediment sent against him by the Scots Parliament, known as the Three Estates. It ended, though, in defeat in 1645 on a field at Philiphaugh in the Borders, where the sharp-faced men of the cloth on the Parliamentary side demanded so much slaughter that the soldiers cried, 'Have you not yet had your fill of blood?' A broken Montrose fled to the continent.

It was to the Scots that Charles eventually surrendered himself. They, in turn, handed him over to Cromwell. However, the king lured them back onto his side with false promises and a Scottish army headed south to free him. The army was smashed but some sections of the Scottish government remained wary of Cromwell, who did his best to win them over once more.

All hope of that was lost when Charles was executed. The Scots merely wanted the monarch brought to heel, they did not want him to lose his head. The Estates immediately proclaimed Charles II king, crowned him at Scone, and positioned themselves in open defiance of Cromwell and the Parliamentarians. Montrose returned but he was defeated and eventually captured in the Highlands. He was brutally executed in Edinburgh.

Despite Montrose's loss, the Scots seemed to be winning. By 1650, Cromwell was in retreat, his men sick and hungry as a scorched earth policy took hold. The Scots commanders wanted to let them go but the religious leaders had other ideas. They wanted more blood. The two forces met at Dunbar, Cromwell seizing the initiative and attacking the much-stronger force with a cry of 'Put your trust in God,

my boys – and keep your powder dry.' The Scots were slaughtered and 5,000 prisoners forced on a death march to Durham. Around 1,500 men died on the way, the survivors herded into the Cathedral to live under brutal conditions. After two months only 1,400 were left to be sold into slavery or sent off to fight in foreign lands.

Following the Dunbar debacle, Charles II decided to ride south with his force in a bid to recapture his throne. He failed and fled into exile.

Meanwhile, Cromwell fought and slaughtered his way through Scotland. Edinburgh, Perth, Stirling, Dundee all fell to him.

Cromwell then ruled the land. When he died in 1658 and Charles II was restored to his throne two years later, peace should have reigned. However, religious differences would soon rise again.

## BLOOD AND GOLD

*The sacking of Dundee by Cromwell's forces in September 1651 was particularly brutal.*

*The army rampaged through the walled city, killing hundreds, including women and children, in one of the bloodiest and least known massacres of the civil wars.*

*Dundee was a repository of gold and it was taken along with other treasures and loaded onto a fleet of 60 ships. The booty did not reach the coffers of Westminster, for the fleet was hit by disaster in the mouth of the Tay – a fierce storm or a devastating fire – and was lost. The treasure still lies somewhere below the waters and has resisted all attempts to find it.*

## SAVING THE TREASURES OF SCOTLAND

*As Cromwell marched north, Scotland's royal regalia of crown, sceptre and mace were placed in Dunottar Castle, nestling on a spit of land on the north east coast.*

*Dunottar Castle, where the Scottish crown was hidden*

*After a siege, the castle was breached but not before the precious artefacts were lowered in a basket to the shoreline below where a servant girl, ostensibly gathering dulse, an edible seaweed, was waiting to spirit them away. They were hidden under the floor of the church at Kinkell until the Reformation. The King's private papers were also smuggled out, sewn into the belt of a woman named Anne Lindsay.*

# Royal blood, holy wars
*Religion leads to the toppling of a dynasty*

L ike his father, Charles II wished to establish his authority over the Scottish Church, who believed in Kirk above King. That kind of notion was heresy to a Stuart monarch and he set out to reform the church in Scotland. The pious Presbyterians naturally took an opposing view and this led to further blood in the fields of Scotland.

Ministers were ejected from their parishes for refusing to follow the King's commands regarding services. They took to the road, many preaching in the open air at what were called conventicles. They and their flock risked imprisonment, slavery and death if caught.

They called them Covenanters, after the Solemn Covenant they signed, and they took up arms against their King. Armies were formed and battles were fought.

But it was the common folk who died during the conflict that saw this period dubbed 'the Killing Times'. The King's forces roamed across south west Scotland, for once the Highlands not being seen as a hotbed of insurrection, and summarily executed anyone who did not swear an oath of allegiance. It is said even simply carrying a Bible could lead to instant death. The area is peppered with memorials to men and women who died where they stood because they refused.

It did not end until Charles died and his brother James became king. But James was a Roman Catholic and even the English did not like that, so he was ousted, William of Orange was brought in, and that, unsurprisingly, led to more bloodshed.

It was James's son, also called James – something that can become most confusing when dealing with the dynasty – who became known as 'The Old Pretender' and it was on his behalf that Jacobites took up arms in 1715 in Scotland. That rebellion was quashed but the toasting of 'the king over the water' continued in secret and many in

Scotland longed for the return of the Stuarts.

Their big chance came in 1745 when James' son, Charles Edward Stuart – Bonnie Prince Charlie – raised his standard at Glenfinnan and announced his bid for the royal title. Highlanders flocked to his side and the army marched southwards, fully intending to reach London. They met with early success but neither a much-hoped for English rebellion nor French reinforcements materialised so the Scottish force reached only as far as Derby before they turned and headed back across the border.

The Jacobite dream ended on 16 April, 1746 near Inverness on Drummossie Moor, better known as Culloden, when the Government forces under the king's son, Prince William Augustus, the Duke of Cumberland (1721–1765), brutally crushed the Jacobites.

Charles Stewart fled the field and ran straight into romantic legend, dodging redcoats, dressing as a woman, taking a boat over the sea to Skye. He eventually reached the beach of Arisaig, where he had landed the year before, and boarded a ship for France. He ended his days on the Continent, drunk, bloated and debauched.

Although a Stuart still sat on a throne in London – Queen Anne, the daughter of James II – the days of the Stuarts as rulers died on the heather and mud of Culloden. The White Cockade that was their symbol withered and died only to be remembered in rose-tinted and drink-fuelled toasts during the next century when the Anglicised nobility rediscovered their Highland

*The clans fell at Culloden*

heritage. Culloden was the final full-scale battle ever fought on British soil.

## MUSIC FOR THE CONQUERING HERO

*The Duke of Cumberland ordered his troops to show the enemy 'No Quarter' at Culloden. That, and the fierce reprisals that followed, earned him the title Bloody Cumberland in Scotland.*

*In England, though, he was a hero and in recognition of his victory, composer George Frideric Handel (1685–1759) was commissioned by the Prince of Wales to write the oratorio 'Judas Maccabeus'. Although there is no direct reference to the Jacobites in the text, its most famous section 'See the Conquering Hero Comes' does reflect the feelings of the ruling classes of the day.*

# Castle Commando
*Learning to kill on the Dark Mile*

Achnacarry Castle has been for generations the ancestral home of the Clan Cameron.

But during World War II it became something else – an academy of death.

In 1940, following the disaster of Dunkirk, Prime Minister Winston Churchill decided that Britain needed its own brand of elite shock troops to harass the enemy – the famed Commando squads.

The rugged and remote Scottish Highlands were deemed the ideal location to induct tough men in the covert skills that made them a breed apart.

There were training camps at Inverary in Argyll and Lochailort but by 1943 Achnacarry had become the Commando Basic Training Centre where Army, Navy and Royal Marine personnel as well as soldiers from occupied countries were hardened into lean, mean, fighting machines.

Turf was concreted over and Nissan huts were erected to house the trainees. Around it was the training ground itself, the so-called Dark Mile.

According to some, the training began as soon as they arrived by train at Spean Bridge, where their belongings were thrown into a lorry and they were marched the seven miles to the castle estate, the ever-present piper at their head. Once at their destination they

*The monument at Spean Bridge*

found a tree-lined avenue with white crosses supposedly memorialising soldiers who had made a fatal error in combat.

Once ensconced in their spartan billet, they had to undergo rigorous training in order to attain the necessary high standards of fitness, daring and lethal acuity. There was an array of speed marches of various length and times – culminating in a march of 15 miles to be completed in under two hours 50 minutes, followed by an assault course and firing practice.

The rugged terrain and vagaries of the Scottish weather helped toughen the men up on cross country marches and periods of living rough, where they learned to live off the land and to conceal themselves. The trainees had no special clothing with which to face the rain, snow, winds, ice cold rivers and swampy heather moors. Meanwhile, instructors acted as snipers and staged ambushes to catch out the unwary.

They had to learn how to scale rockfaces and build makeshift rope bridges. They strengthened their bodies with brutal exercise, including tossing and catching large tree trunks. They learned how to kill quickly and silently.

A flotilla of varying types of craft was stored on nearby Loch Lochy and here the Commandos took part in mock night raids, during which they had to cross the water and then attack an emplacement. As with the sniper attacks and ambushes on the speed marches, live ammunition and explosives were used. These weapons were in the capable hands of instructors who knew how to shoot without hitting anything, even under such conditions.

Those who showed they had the right stuff to be part of the new Special Forces squad earned the right to wear the famed Green Beret.

They were dropped by parachute or landed by sea. They fought across Europe and Asia, in small groups or as part of larger forces, as in the D-Day landings, when they waded ashore on Sword Beach.

They won 38 battle honours and eight Victoria Crosses. Sadly, 1,700

of them died and many more were wounded.

In 1952, the Queen Mother unveiled a dramatic monument near to Spean Bridge. It shows three commandos looking towards the mountains with the motto 'United We Conquer' carved from the stone base.

## The bandit masquerading as a Scottish officer
*The kilted killer with a price on his head*

Major Tommy MacPherson was a commando – and extremely daring.

Born in Edinburgh, he became known as the Kilted Killer and had a bounty of 300,000 French francs placed on his head by the occupying Germans, who called him a 'bandit masquerading as a Scottish officer.'

He had been parachuted into France to aid the French Resistance, the Maquis, to disrupt the occupying forces. He proved very adept at both sabotage, killing and getting under the Nazi High Command's skin.

He also took to driving around in a black Citroen with a Union flag and Cross of Lorraine flying in full view.

Even before he landed in France, MacPherson had already distinguished himself in North Africa, been a prisoner-of-war, and serial escapee.

His final escape, from a camp in Poland, was successful and he returned to Scotland but was recruited by the SOE (Special Operations Executive, Churchill's secret army, which had been ordered to set Europe ablaze).

They sent him to France as part of Operation Jedburgh to cause as much mayhem as he could in the lead up to the Normandy landings.

His story is filled with adventure and derring-do. He was brave and daring and audacious.

On one occasion he managed to convince a German commander to surrender with an outrageous bluff. He convinced him that he was in direct contact with London and with one word could summon an air strike that would blast the 1,000 strong German force off the earth. The truth was MacPherson had only a handful of men at his back. However, the ruse worked and the Germans surrendered without a shot fired.

With France free of the Nazis, MacPherson should have been able to relax but he was sent into Northern Italy where he again harried the Germans but also found himself in opposition to Yugoslavia's Marshall Tito and his Communist Partisans who had eyes on the territory.

Major MacPherson received many honours and commendations during his swashbuckling career. In 2010 he published his memoirs, *Behind Enemy Lines*, and he died in 2014.

# Here we go round the Mulberry
*The Scottish village that was vital to D-Day Landings*

One of the greatest secrets of World War II was the floating harbours used effectively during D-Day.

They called them Mulberries – and a small coastal village nestling on Wigtown Bay in the South-West of Scotland became vital to their success. The temporary harbours were used to off-load cargo from as far as a mile out to sea in order to support the allied push into Normandy.

Naturally, the project was incredibly hush-hush, with prototypes being made in Wales and then floated up to Scotland for testing. The codename Mulberry was selected for no other reason than it was next on the list!

The small planned village of Garlieston, founded by Lord Garlies in the mid-18th century, was selected as the test area. The beaches in the vicinity were deemed most like the invasion points the allies could expect to find at Normandy – flat and sandy, with similar tides, as well as remote enough to ensure security.

Locals were moved out and the land around the village was declared a no-go area. A camp was established at Cairnhead to house the workers, engineers and military personnel needed to make the tests.

The final design was for a series of floating pierheads linked by steel roadways. Around 45,000 workers on the Thames and the Clyde were then involved in construction with additional work in Wales. They were towed to Garlieston where the vital sea trials were carried out.

Various sections of the floating harbours had unique names – swiss roll, for the wooden walkway

*The memorial erected in 1995 at Garlieston*

which was later abandoned, beetles (floating pontoons), crocodiles (roadway) and hippos (caissons, or water supports).

The Germans had, over two years and using forced labour, constructed immense harbour defences from concrete and steel. The Allies got round them by bringing their own harbours. It was, as German engineer and designer Albert Speer said, 'An idea of simple genius.'

A granite memorial was erected in the village in 1995 to commemorate its unique contribution to the war effort.

## THE LONGEST ECHO

*A gun fired in a Ross-shire fuel dump resulted in the world's longest echo.*

*The Inchindown oil storage tanks, near Invergordon, were hacked out on Kinrive Hill just before World War II to store 32 million gallons of fuel. The tunnel complex was the largest single construction project in Scotland since the Caledonian Canal and was in use until the Falklands War in 1982.*

*The longest echo record was smashed there in 2014 when scientists found that a gunshot took 75 seconds to die. The previous record was 15 seconds, made by the closing of a door in the Hamilton Mausoleum, South Lanarkshire.*

# BUILDING A COUNTRY

Scotland's landscape can present difficult challenges for engineers and has led to some incredible innovation.

## The Northeast Passage
*Building the Caledonian Canal*

In the late 18th and 19th century, the UK Government became aware of the problems of depopulation and unemployment in the Highlands.

Highlanders were emigrating at too swift a rate for comfort. Some did so willingly, others forcibly moved from the glens and hillsides by lairds more interested in profit than the wellbeing of the people.

In 1803 work began on an ambitious and costly project that would link the west with the east and provide a shipping route to the east coast that avoided the dangerous west coast waters and the hazards of Cape Wrath.

The Caledonian Canal was to run for 60 miles from near Fort William to Inverness, through some spectacular scenery. It would follow the line of the Great Glen (also known as Glen More or Glen Albyn), a fault line that bisects the Northwestern portion of Scotland from the rest of the country. The canal would link the series of lochs that spread along the glen – Dochfour, Lochy, Oich and Ness – with Loch Linnhe that opens to the Firth of Lorne and then on to the Atlantic and the Moray Firth that opens on the North Sea. That meant only around 22 miles of actual canal had to be dug, although one loch had to be artificially raised.

Around 3,000 workers braved the rugged terrain and the full force of the Scottish weather to hack out the land for the canal sections and to construct the 29 locks needed to raise and lower vessels along the way. Ironically, as a work creation scheme for local men, the workforce had to be augmented by Irish labourers.

The section known as Neptune's Staircase, a series of eight locks and a sea lock to bring the canal level

*The bridge Telford constructed
at Dunkeld in Perthshire*

with Loch Linnhe, is one of the
longest combinations of locks in the
country and can take 90 minutes to
get through.

Thanks to the system, sailors
crossing the Laggan section
between Lochs Oich and Lochy can
amaze themselves with the thought
that they are actually 105 feet above
sea level.

A budget of £474,000 (over
£15m today) was set aside for the
work, which was originally to have
been completed in seven years. But
that ballooned to £840,000 (over
£38m today) as the project came
in five years behind schedule – and
even then there was further work
needed between 1844 and 1849,
due to storm damage and the

collapse of shoddy materials.

As for the depopulation, it
continued unabated throughout
the 19th century as rich
landowners continued to clear
the land of people in order to
make way for more profitable
sheep and shooting pursuits.

The Caledonian Canal may
never have achieved its potential
commercially or militarily, although
during World War I it was used by
vessels seeking to avoid the German
warships preying on the north coast
of Scotland. It is an impressive feat
nonetheless.

Queen Victoria visited the canal
in 1873. Tourism was beginning to
take shape and southerners were
introduced to the attractions of
the canal and the scenic wonders
through which it cuts, assisted by
the growth of the railways which
had reached both Fort William at
the southern end and Inverness
to the north. Commercial tour
boats took to the waters in the
1930s and the canal increased
even more in popularity.

In 1995 it was closed by owners
British Waterways for upgrading

work to be carried out and reopened ten years later. It is now a busy waterway for both leisure and commercial craft and draws visitors from all over the world.

## THE MAN WITH THE PLAN

*The man entrusted with planning the Caledonian Canal was engineer Thomas Telford (1757–1834). The son of a Borders shepherd, he trained as a stone mason and built the Ellesmere Canal, connecting the Severn with the Mersey, as well as around 1,000 miles of roadways and 100 bridges across the country.*

*In the end, due to economies, the Highland waterway was not as deep as he'd imagined and was seen as something of a failure. During the years of construction ships had changed so much that the canal could not accommodate them.*

*He went on to build the suspension bridge across the Menai Straits and the Conway Bridge and died in 1834.*

## FULL STEAM AHEAD

*The Caledonian Canal may have been Thomas Telford's legacy but it might never have come to fruition if it wasn't for Greenock-born James Watt (1736–1819).*

*It was Watt who, in 1773, surveyed the area with a view to an inland waterway being built.*

*However, it was his idea of perfecting steam engines by inventing the separate condenser and air pump that had the most impact. It ushered in the industrial age, for not only was the then amazing steam dredger used to help gouge out the canals but it also helped make the canal itself almost obsolete thanks to the arrival of steamers which tackled the rough seas and strong winds of the west coast and northern sea routes.*

*However, it was the steam train that gave the canal its tourism lifeline in the latter half of the 19th century.*

Steam pioneer James Watt

# Big wheel keep on rollin'

*The lock system that proved daunting*

The Caledonian Canal's Neptune's Staircase may be a long process to get through but the eleven locks linking the Forth & Clyde and Union Canals at Falkirk could take almost a day!

The Union Canal was originally designed as a means to bring cheaper fuel from the West of Scotland.

The locks that linked it with the commercial waterway that was the Forth & Clyde were dismantled in 1933 and the use of canals in Scotland died out.

However, by the 1990s there was renewed interest in the inland waterways for leisure and the thorny problem of how to move craft from one canal to the other was revisited.

A variety of solutions were considered, including tanks that tilted, a seesaw, an overhead monorail and a rolling egg design. Finally, a giant, 35-metre (114 feet)

tall wheel system was decided upon – the world's first rotating boat lift - and the design was said to have been inspired by, variously, a Celtic double-headed spear, a whale's ribcage, a revolving propeller and a fish spine.

Work on the £84m project began in 1998, with over 1,000 workers involved in its construction. Parts were manufactured in Derbyshire then taken by road to Falkirk. A total of 1,200 tonnes of steel were used while a total of 15,000 nuts were each hand tightened. Each 600 tonne gondola can hold 500,000 litres of water. Amazingly, it requires only a minimal amount of energy to make it turn – the equivalent of boiling eight kettles of water.

*The Falkirk Wheel*

The Falkirk Wheel was opened by the Queen in 2002, linking the two refurbished canals for the first time in 70 years, and it is now one of the area's major tourist attractions.

## THE CANAL THAT ALMOST NEVER WAS

*The Forth & Clyde was conceived as a vital waterway between the two great rivers – but cash flow problems almost sank it without trace. Finally, Jacobite cash allowed it to reach its destination.*

*Work began in 1768 at what is now Grangemouth on the Forth but shovels were downed seven years later just north of Glasgow. Glasgow businessmen raised funds two years later to allow the army of navvies to get back to work – but only as far as the city. In 1785, money that had been seized by the Government from Jacobite lords allowed the enterprise to reach Bowling on the Clyde. It was officially opened in 1790.*

# The road to peace
*The transport project designed to pacify the Highlands*

In 1724, Irish-born Major General George Wade (1673–1748) was sent to Scotland to report back to his commanders about the state of affairs in Scotland. He estimated there were around 12,000 heavily armed Highlanders lurking in the hills and the valleys ready to take up the cause once again. They could move through the heather and the mountain passes with ease but the land was less welcoming for the military boot. Wade proposed that a series of roads and bridges be built to link the forts in order to improve communications, speed up transport and generally make it easier for the army to root out these dangerous enemies of the state.

On 10 May, 1725 he was promoted to Commander in Chief Northern Britain (Scotland then not a name being used lest it lead to any pesky notions of division) and he set out on his ambitious plan to forge new routes into the Highlands. It was a vast undertaking and on a scale not attempted since the Romans tried to make inroads into this hostile territory. Wade, though, was significantly more successful.

Using soldiers, and Highlanders in need of wages, as labourers, he oversaw the construction of around 300 miles of roadway and 40 bridges over the next 15 years. The first stretch lay between Fort William and Fort Augustus. The roads were 4.8 metres (sixteen feet) wide with camps every ten miles, where inns often sprang up, for soldiers were thirsty men. The most notable bridge is perhaps the one at Aberfeldy with its five arches and is still known as General Wade's Bridge.

During his time as Commander in Chief, he raised a militia from clans loyal to the crown. Known as the Highland Watches, these ten companies of men were amalgamated in 1739 and were given the name the Black Watch. In the years after the '45 rebellion, when the Proscription Acts were enforced to stamp out the Highland way of life, they were the only force permitted by law to sport the tartan.

The great roadbuilding project was continued by Major William Caulfeild (1698–1767), who managed to spur the workforce to lay down over 800 miles, although that did take 27 years.

Militarily, the roads were a success but as the threat of hostilities eased during the 19th century many of the lesser roads fell into disuse because neither central nor local government wished to maintain them. Some of the system had been drawn into the routes used by Thomas Telford and, indeed, are still in use today. Many parts of the modern A9 still follow the same route of the Wade road north and it is there you can see one of his marker stones, known as the Wade Stone.

### CRUSHING LYRICS

*Wade's work was highly regarded by his superiors. So much so that his name appears in an original verse of a song first performed in 1745 that would later become the National Anthem of the United Kingdom:*

**Lord, grant that Marshal Wade,**
**May by thy mighty aid,**
**Victory bring.**
**May he sedition hush and like a torrent rush,**
**Rebellious Scots to crush,**
**God save the King.**

---

# Planes, Trains – and trains that are planes
*The futuristic idea that never took off*

George Bennie (1891–1957) should be a household name today. He had an idea that was ahead of its time – a means of transport that would provide high-speed travel for the masses and protect the environment. But the Railplane, a propeller-driven monorail system, did not receive the financial backing it needed and its visionary inventor died in obscurity.

Glasgow-born Bennie was the son of an engineer but not qualified himself. He had a fascination with transport and he built a prototype above a railway track in Milngavie in 1930.

On 8 July, the press and public saw a bullet-shaped carriage suspended on a rail with electric propellers front and aft. The carriage was stabilised by wheels on another track which stood about 3.6 metres (12 feet) off the ground. It was, it was noted, like something out of a Flash Gordon film.

Inside the conditions were luxurious. Passengers walked on lush carpets, sat on the comfortable seats and the windows were curtained. There were lamps on the tables. And the doors slid open and closed, like a lift.

Bennie claimed his Railplane would reach speeds of 120mph (193kph) but no-one ever witnessed that. The test track was a mere 120 metres (393 feet) long and it is unlikely that it achieved anything higher than 50mph (80kph).

However, everything on the showpiece journey went well and the passengers were sufficiently impressed by the smoothness of the ride, with no smoke belching from an engine, no clattering over rails, no noisy whistles.

But despite the idea of a Glasgow to Edinburgh line being suggested, and another between Blackpool and Southport, the Bennie Railplane got no further than that 120 metres (393 feet) in Milngavie. Investors stayed away and, it has been suggested, that dirty work by rail owners was in play.

Bennie was declared bankrupt in 1937 but he refused to give up. He formed new companies and tried to sell his idea to Middle Eastern concerns but again failed.

His test track and the luxurious carriage lay ignored until the 1950s when it was sold for scrap.

Bennie himself abandoned his dreams and opened a herbalist store which he operated until his death in 1957.

# Rocket science
*The air mail idea that prosved explosive*

Scarp, a small island off the coast of Harris in the Hebrides, is uninhabited now but that wasn't always the case. Once, around 200 people scratched a life from the land but by the 1970s the last of the families left the island to the seabirds, the wind and the rain.

But 40 years before, it was deemed ideal for an experiment that would become known as *Lathan a Rocait* – the Day of the Rocket.

It was the brainchild of Gerhard Zucker (1908–1985), who had left his native Germany under something of a cloud, having failed to interest the Nazi government in his belief that rockets could be used to transport mail. What he didn't know was that they were already secretly working on their own rocket fuel, but with more sinister aims. Zucker's own rockets were little more than a hull powered by gunpowder, rather like fireworks. His experiments in his homeland had failed to cover him in the glory he'd expected and so he came to Britain hoping to attract investment and interest the authorities.

His first two attempts over land in England met with some success and did manage to at least pique the attention of the British Government. Next they had to test Zucker's rockets over water – and Scarp was selected as the launching pad.

The idea was to fire the device across the half-mile sound between the island and Harris, landing on Hushinish Point. Rocket mail, said Zucker, would be a boon to the Western Isles, making communication almost immediate.

If it worked, the service could help in situations such as that faced by Christina Maclennan. Expecting twins, she gave birth to one daughter in her Scarp home on 13 January, 1934 but the unborn sibling was causing problems. There was no doctor, just an 85-year-old woman who acted as midwife, and no telephone to call for help. Mrs Maclennan had to be taken 50 miles across the choppy sound by

*The commemorative Rocket Post stamp*

ferry, then on the floor of a bus and finally by private car to reach the hospital in Stornoway, where the second child was born two days later. Some means of high-speed communication might have helped the situation.

The rocket was launched on 28 July, 1934. It was packed with 1200 letters, one even to King George V, and special stamps were printed. Once the rocket landed, the letters would be collected and delivered.

The rocket didn't land – it exploded in the air, shredding much of its load. The remainder of the post fluttered to the ground. Three days later, an undeterred Zucker tried again, this time in the opposite direction – from Harris to Scarp. Once again it exploded, spraying the charred remains of letters across the beach.

The British Government decided Zucker was a threat to national security and sent him back to Germany. Once home he was arrested, he claimed for high treason but the truth may be that the authorities thought he was guilty of fraud and embezzlement in regard to selling fake postal covers for his rocket launches. He spent 16 months in jail.

He served in the Luftwaffe during the war and in the 1960s resumed his rocketry experiments, one of which resulted in fatalities when the rocket again exploded. The West German government promptly banned all civilian rocket research.

Zucker's story, however, lived on. Letters showing burn marks can be seen in the local museum in Harris while the 2006 film *The Rocket Post* told a largely fictionalised version.

## BLAST OFF

*The Hebridean connection with rockets did not end with Zucker's disastrous experiments. A missile base was established on South Uist in 1957/1958, despite some local opposition.*

*On 21 August, 1998 the first unmanned aircraft landed at the range, having taken off from Newfoundland the previous day.*

*It was from the range, in October 2015, that the first rocket was launched into space from UK soil. The US Terrier-Orion two-stage rocket was treated as a ballistic missile and left the earth's atmosphere before it was blown up over the Atlantic as a part of an international military exercise.*

*Author Sir Compton Mackenzie wrote a comic novel in 1957 based on the opposition to the scheme. Called* **Rockets Galore**, *it was a sequel to his classic* **Whisky Galore**. *However, it did not find similar success.*

## THE POWER OF MUSIC

*The first hydro-electric scheme in Scotland was created to power an organ! In 1890, the monks at Fort Augustus Abbey on the shores of Loch Ness built the 18kw device. It not only kept the instrument going, it also generated street lighting for the village.*

*However, it's been claimed that when the organ played, the lights dimmed.*

# The men who made the Hollow Mountain
*Bringing power to the people*

They were called 'Tunnel Tigers' and they hacked and drilled and blasted in order to hollow out a mountain to provide power for homes and businesses 100 miles away.

The men, numbered variously at between 1,300 and 3,000, transformed Ben Cruachan in Argyll into a hidden power station to create what is one of the most impressive feats of engineering the world has ever seen. But it was not without its cost in human lives.

The project cost £24.5m (around half a billion today) and had been guided through Parliament in 1943 by Secretary of State for Scotland, Tom Johnston (1881–1965), swimming against the tide of rich landowners who wanted to block it. The Red Clydesider was passionate about the future of hydro power, not simply as a means of keeping homes warm and businesses moving but also as a way to create employment in a post-war market that was looking decidedly bleak for many.

The work began in 1959 and continued until 1965 and workers flooded into the area around Loch Awe, over which the twin peaks of Cruachan stands, to fill hotels, boarding houses and specially constructed camps.

The Tunnel Tigers gouged out 220,000 cubic metres of granite with hand-held air drills and blasted it away with gelignite to create a cavern large enough to house a cathedral or the Tower of London, as well as a warren of passageways and corridors. The noise from the drills, the blasting and the heavy machinery was deafening. The perils of dust, debris and flying stones took their toll. And over it all was the overpowering stench of diesel fumes.

But all the motorists on the busy tourist route at the foot of the mountain knows about it is the signs advertising the visitor centre and, further up the Pass of Brander, the massive dam.

A small cairn on the lochside tells a more poignant story, for it memorialises the 36 men who died during construction. In the machine room hall deep within the mountain there is another memorial specifically to the 15 men who perished underground.

It was dangerous work and one group of workers, who drilled a vertical shaft, was known as the Suicide Squad. One colleague recalled that their pay slips were stamped with the words 'Danger money'. One died when he fell 152 metres (500 feet).

In another incident, three men

*Ben Cruachan towers behind Loch Awe*

perished when there was an accident during the concreting of a pipe.

And one death, it is whispered, may not have been an accident at all. A gambler, who kept his own book of gambling debts, was crushed to death. But later there were the hidden problems – hearing loss, breathing difficulties, emphysema.

The pay, with or without danger money, was good – more than the men could command elsewhere, even within the hydro-electricity industry. But the invasion of workers had an impact on the rural community.

The men worked hard and they needed to play hard, their life given an edge by the dangers they faced.

The local pubs and hotels were filled on Friday and Saturday nights. The men would then stagger back on foot to the Nissan huts they called home. There was drinking. There was gambling. There was womanising. Sometimes tensions overflowed and there were bar-room brawls. Some of the stories would not be out of place in a western film.

Finally, the complex was opened by the Queen on 15 October, 1965, although only one of the massive machines was on-line. Another was not operational until 1966 and the third in 1967.

## PUMPED UP

*The electrical storage system within the hollow mountain, known as a reversible pump storage system, was the first in the world to be built on such a scale.*

*Basically, the water flows down from the man-made loch high up the mountain-side, generates and stores energy for use during peak times, and then is pumped back up again overnight*

*to begin the process again.*

*To generate the power to keep the lights burning, the workers at Ben Cruachan had to build two dams (one a massive 316 metres (1,037 feet) long) and 13 aqueducts as well as construct power lines and generating stations.*

## THE RECORD-BREAKING ROCK BREAKERS

*Forty-five Irish workers employed on the hydro-electric scheme in St Fillans, Perthshire broke a record in 1955.*

*They worked round-the-clock to hack their way through an astonishing 169 metres (557 feet) of solid rock in just one week. In other words, using only hand-held drills, they dug through the height of the Blackpool Tower. They received a bonus for their labours – £20.*

*Power giant SSE opened a new visitor centre in Pitlochry, Perthshire in 2017 which commemorates the scheme and the men who put their lives on the line.*

## Bridges over the River Forth
*Three icons in bridge-making*

There are three bridges standing side-by-side across the River Forth and each is iconic.

Construction of the latest, the Queensferry Crossing, began in 2011 and was completed six years later, at a cost of around £1.35 billion. At 1.7 miles long (2.7km) it is the world's longest three-tower, cable-stayed bridge and was built to alleviate the heavy traffic between Edinburgh in the south to the Kingdom of Fife.

It forms part of a 13.7 mile (22km) overhaul to the motorway system, known as the Forth Replacement Crossing scheme, which sees the first ever use of variable mandatory speed limits and a dedicated bus lane on the hard shoulder in Scotland.

It also boasts wind baffles to help combat the fierce gusts that can roar in from the North Sea, cutting down on the number of closures due to weather.

The existing Forth Road Bridge has been regularly hit by such closures since it opened in 1964. The opening of the new bridge meant it could be dedicated to public transport, cycling and walking.

The road crossing had been planned for decades but the economic crises of the 1930s and then the outbreak of World War II saw them shelved. Construction finally began in September 1958 with three British firms forming a consortium for the successful bid.

When it opened in 1964 it was not only the world's most northerly long-span suspension bridge but also the longest suspension bridge outside the USA.

Tens of thousands of people crammed along shorelines on that misty September day for the opening ceremony by the Queen, while the Royal Navy fired a 21-gun salute from vessels moored in the Forth.

Originally a toll bridge – 20,000 half crowns were taken within three and a half hours of the official opening. The tolls were used to pay back the government loan of

*The iconic Bridge over the Forth*

£14.5 million needed to meet the £19.5 million total costs. The bridge was an instant success and carried an average of 24 million vehicles across it and the debt was met in December 1993. Tolls were abolished by the Scottish Government in 2008.

The bridge itself was granted Category A Listed Building status in 2001 in recognition of its achievement in engineering.

For decades prior to its opening, the only way across this section of the Forth was by rail via the iconic Forth Bridge, which itself replaced the ferry. Opening in 1890, it had taken seven years to construct, employing 5,000 tradesmen and labourers working 54,000 tonnes of steel, 20,950 cubic metres of granite, 6,780 cubic metres of stone, 49,200 cubic metres of concrete, 50 tonnes of cement and seven million rivets.

It had, in its day, the world's longest spans, at 541 metres (1,775 feet) and at a length of 2,539 metres (8,297 feet) it remains one of the world's longest cantilever bridges. The bridge now carries around 200 trains every day.

The entire cantilever structure

was refurbished between 1998 and 2011 and saw an average of 400 people a day employed on cleaning, repairing, restoration and upgrading.

In 2015 the Category A Listed structure was declared a UNESCO World Heritage Site.

## THE DISASTER THAT KILLED A REPUTATION

*A major rail disaster led to the original plans for the Forth Bridge to be abandoned.*

*The Tay Rail Bridge was opened in June 1878 and was the longest bridge in the world. On 28 December, 1879, violent winds caused it to collapse, sending a passenger train plunging into the icy waters and killing 75 people.*

*The designer, Thomas Bouch, had been knighted for his achievements and work had begun on his Forth bridge design but that was shelved. His son-in-law was among those who died. Bouch was held responsible for the disaster and, with his reputation in tatters, he died in 1880.*

## THE HIDDEN COST OF BRIDGE BUILDING

*It took over a century to be made public, but finally it was revealed that at least 73 men died in constructing the Forth Bridge.*

*Officially, 57 deaths of the men known as 'briggers' were acknowledged. It took years of detective work by members of the Forth Bridge Memorial Committee to reveal the true figure, although it may be even higher.*

*The first casualty was 16-year-old Thomas Harris, who fell from the jetty in 1883.*

*Bridge-building was dangerous work and some of the men who died may have suffered from 'the bends' during construction of the caissons deep into the Forth. Seven men died in building the Forth Road Bridge but only one tragedy occurred during construction of the new crossing.*

## THE WORLD'S TALLEST CINEMA

*Glasgow was once known as Cinema City because of its high proportion of picture houses. Now the city has another film-related claim to fame – it is home to the tallest cinema in the world.*

*The 18-screen building in Renfrew Street is 62 metres (203 feet) high, with theatres on six levels, and was built in 2003. It was voted Scotland's ugliest building with a Carbuncle of the Year, an annual award handed out for architecture and the degeneration of towns, because it was deemed too big to fit comfortably into its surroundings.*

*It soon became the busiest cinema in Britain and is now part of the Cineworld chain.*

# THIS SPORTING LIFE

Scotland has a fine sporting tradition. It is the recognised home of golf, perhaps even football, and it has given Britain a tennis hero in Sir Andy Murray.

## War Games
*The show of strength that became sport*

The Highland Games of today mix colour and spectacle with feats of strength, all underscored by the skirl of the pipes, the throb of the drums and the sound of dancing feet. It is as much part of Scotland as the haggis, the bagpipes and the kilt.

But like many other things traditionally Scottish, it may have originated in Ireland, and crossed the water when the Dalriadic Scots invaded in the fourth and fifth centuries.

The games are, essentially, war games, designed to identify the strongest, most able warriors. The 'heavy events' are most noticeably rooted in war, for they seek champions who can throw heavy objects the furthest. For instance, the original cabers would be tree trunks, the shot putt large stones.

When King Malcolm Canmore, who defeated Macbeth to reign from 1057 to 1093, needed a new royal messenger, he summoned the fleetest of foot to stage a race up Craig Coinnich near Braemar. This may well have been the earliest beginnings of what are now the largest games in Scotland – the famed Braemar Gathering, held every September.

As the tests of strength and

*Show of strength at the Highland Games*

manhood progressed, piping competitions were added, for the clan chiefs liked to pit their musicians against their rivals. Fiddles and the Highland harp, the *clarsach*, also were popular, while Highland dancing became a stalwart event.

The oldest games are said to be the Ceres Games in Fife, which began in 1314 when Robert the Bruce granted the locals a charter to hold a market and fair as a thanks for their help at the battle of Bannockburn.

However, following the disaster of Culloden and the imposition of the Proscription Acts in 1746, the crackdown on all things Highland meant that such gatherings were deemed illegal.

It wasn't until the visit by George IV in 1822 that Highland culture began to be accepted, largely due to the efforts of Sir Walter Scott. It was the first visit to Scotland of a reigning monarch since James VI (James I of England). Scott had made a fortune out of romanticising Scotland's past and he brought that flair to the fore for the visit.

The Scottish diaspora took

the games to new worlds. The first games in the United States were held in New York in 1836 while they spread across the continent to Canada. Australia and New Zealand also mark their Scottish links with events.

# An unprofitable sport
*Golf – the game the Scots gave to the world*

The idea of hitting a ball with a stick dates back to Roman times, perhaps even earlier. The Romans had a game called *paganica*, in which players did just that. The Chinese had a version, while it is known that the Dutch and the Belgians also used a curved stick to beat a ball about.

However, it is widely accepted that the modern game of golf – or gowff, as it was known, perhaps from the Dutch word *colf* for 'stick' – was devised in Scotland. The oldest course in the world is the Old Links in Musselburgh, although it only has nine holes. However, it was in Scotland that the rules of playing an 18-hole game were set down.

It was a sport of kings and queens. Mary, Queen of Scots played, for it was noted that she had a tendency towards sports that were deemed unladylike, although this could refer to her love of football. She enjoyed a round on the Musselburgh links only days after the murder of her husband, Lord Darnley, and set tongues wagging in the process. It is said that, in her younger days, she introduced the game to France, and from this we get the word 'caddie', for her French aides were known as cadets. However, the term caddie was used in Scotland for anyone who acted as a porter, so it is more likely it stems from that.

Not all monarchs were enamoured of the game, though. They believed that it, and other sports, tended to get in the way of the serious business of killing the enemy. Golf and football were banned a number of times because they distracted the men from archery practice. In 1457, it was ordered that golf be '*utterly cryit doun and not usit.*' Another ban decreed that '*futbawis, gowff or uther six unproffitable sportis'* not be played.

The bans didn't last, for James IV was known to enjoy the game, while it was James VI and I of the United Kingdom who took it to London when he acceded to the throne of England.

The first set of rules were set down on paper by the Honourable Company of Edinburgh Golfers in 1744 when they played the very first organised competition. Ten years later, the St Andrews Society of Golfers was formed and in 1764 they reduced the course from 22 holes to 18. In 1834 they received the title 'Royal & Ancient' from William IV.

In 1860, the very first Open Championship was played in Prestwick. Fittingly, it was won by a Scot, Willie Park Snr.

In recent years controversy has dogged some clubs over their policy of not allowing female members. It was as late as 2014 before the R&A voted to change the rules and the following year the first woman, Angela Bonallack, played in a match as a member. One ancient club, Muirfield in Edinburgh, had its

*The modern game was developed in Scotland*

right to host Open Championships taken from it when the all-male membership voted against allowing women into their ranks. Women could play on the links and visit the clubhouse, but only as guests. One year after that vote, another ballot was taken and this time it was decided that women could join the club after all. Although it was pointed out that it might take two or three years before the first female appeared on the membership roster due to a lengthy waiting list.

The game, of course, now covers the globe and has come a long way from when Fife folk used to batter pebbles across sand dunes with a crooked stick.

## IN THE FORE FRONT

*A game in 1684 provides one explanation for the warning 'Fore!' The Duke of York – later James II of the UK – took exception to two English noblemen claiming that the game was a southern invention. He joined local golfer and ballmaker John Patterson and challenged the impertinent duo to a match on Leith Links. Naturally, Scotland won and Patterson, with a generous share of the winnings, was able to build a house on Edinburgh's Canongate which he called 'Golfer's Land.'*

*The players would shout a warning to their 'fore-caddies', who stood where the ball was intended to land in order to cut down on the number lost. Over time, this was shortened to simply 'Fore!'*

## IN THE NEWS

*The first golf match to be reported in a newspaper took place on Leith Links in 1724 when Captain John Porteous played the Honourable Alexander Elphinstone before a large crowd.*

*The 'solemn match of golf', as the newspaper called it, was played for a stake of twenty guineas (£22). Elphinstone won.*

*Five years later, Elphinstone was back in the news – but for a more deadly game. He fought a duel on the Links with an army officer, who later died of his wounds, and it seemed Elphinstone would face charges but in the end skated free.*

*Captain Porteous was not so fortunate. A lynch mob hung him in the Grassmarket for ordering his Town Guard to fire on an unruly crowd during an unpopular execution.*

## Sticking it to the warriors
*Preparing for battle with stick and ball*

Golf is not the only Scottish sport that involves hitting a ball with a stick. Shinty was probably imported to Scotland from Ireland with the Celtic missionaries and may well have been devised as a form of keeping the tribe's warriors prepared for battle.

In matches, teams of 12 players have to propel a small leather ball into goal to score. Prior to leather being used, the balls might have been made from wood or even dried cow pats.

In Scotland the game is played mainly in the Highlands with the curved wooden stick called a *caman*, leading to the Gaelic name for the sport, *Camanachd*. In times past, in places where wood was scarce, dried seawood stalks were used to fashion the *caman*.

Unlike hockey, players can hit the ball in mid-air and can use both sides of the *caman*. They can block and tackle shoulder-to-shoulder but can't hack – bring their *caman* down on an opponent's. The goalkeeper can use his open hands and hitting the ball with the head is deemed a foul, and not recommended.

Two international matches were played against Ireland in Dublin and Glasgow (using the ground of Celtic FC) during 1896/97. Scotland won both.

Just after World War II, Murrayfield, the home of Scottish rugby in Edinburgh, hosted a match between Newtonmore and Ballachullish. This become known as the 'pots and pans' match because, due to a lack of silver for trophies, the teams competed for a prize of cooking ware. Newtonmore won and the prizes headed to the Cairngorm village. When the National Museum of Scotland asked to borrow them for an exhibition, they had to wait until they were washed out, as the holder's wife had made a pot of soup in them.

*A caman, used in shinty*

Newtonmore's fiercest rivals are Kingussie – a village only three miles away. The latter has been named as the most successful team in the sport.

In 2014, Shinty arrived in Russia when a locally formed club, Krasnodar Camanchd, organised a match – with themselves.

It is also believed that when Scots headed to Canada to make a new life for themselves during the Clearances, they took Shinty with them – and eventually it transformed into Ice Hockey.

### THE ROYAL BALL

*One of the oldest known footballs in existence was found in Scotland. The ball, half the size of its modern equivalent, was found in Stirling Castle in 1999 behind panelling in the bedchamber of Mary, Queen of Scots. It was made of a pig's bladder encased in cow hide and was dated to around 1540, although it could be much older. It is recorded that James IV bought four 'fut ballis' in 1497. Could this ball be one of them?*

*Mary was in the habit of throwing the ball from her balcony to the players waiting below. No one is quite certain how it came to be lodged behind the panels.*

## The not so beautiful game
*Hooligans meant business*

The warring families of the borderlands between Scotland and England were prone to taking football hooliganism to extremes. The matches themselves could be fierce, bloody affairs.

In 1599, a six-a-side match was organised between players from the Scottish Armstrong family and a side from Bewcastle, just over the border in Cumbria. The game was played, although who won has not been recorded for posterity. However, as was the custom, both sides retired to a local inn for some refreshments.

A local man, William Ridley, wished to punish the Armstrongs for previous depredations, the Borders being particularly violent during these times, and gathered together some friends to ambush them. Unfortunately he must have told the wrong person for the Armstrongs were prepared. The English gang found itself surrounded by 200 fierce riders. During the resulting bloodshed three of the English were killed, including Ridley, while many others were 'sore hurt'. The latter included one John Whitfield 'whose bowels came out but are sowed up againe.' The Armstrongs took thirty other prisoners for later ransom.

Thirty years before, the north of England was the scene for another match, this time with royalty among the spectators.

It was in June 1568, while Mary, Queen of Scots was being held in Carlisle after she fled her own country, that she watched a two-hour game on the meadow below the castle between twenty of her own staff. Trees at either end of the makeshift pitch were used as goalposts.

Francis Hepburn, the Earl of

Bothwell (1562–1612), nephew of Queen Mary's lover and eventual husband, was also fond of a kickabout, in every sense of the word. During one match in 1592, the tough guy Earl was playing a game with other Border freebooters and was kicked on the leg by another nobleman. Kick came to shove and soon the two men were ready to take the matter further the following day with something more lethal than a ball. However, the king intervened and tempers were cooled to prevent a foul becoming foul play.

## NET RESULT FOR MONARCHS

*The oldest tennis courts still in use can be found in Fife. King James V (1512–1542) was a fan of the game and had them created at Falkland Palace.*

*They can still be seen today very much as the King would have seen them, and played on them, after their two years of construction.*

*Both keen sportswoman Mary, Queen of Scots and her son James VI have swung a racquet on the two courts, although it is not known if royal tempers flared with any outburst of 'Thou hast got to be kidding!'*

# Sport on the slide
*Brushing up on curling*

It numbers Hollywood star George Clooney among its fans, dates back over 400 years at least and proved a big hit at the Winter Olympics.

Curling, something like bowls on ice with vigorous brushing to make the stone slide faster, has been recorded in Scotland since the 16th century.

It was in 1541 that the first mention was made of a game played on some ice at Paisley Abbey between a monk and a kinsman of his Abbot. It became popular in Scotland and emigrants took the game abroad, particularly Canada, which saw, in 1807, the establishment of the oldest sporting club in North America – The Royal Montreal Curling Club. The sport also spread quickly across the USA, and is now popular in China.

Robert Burns even mentions the sport, in his poem *Tam Samson's Elegy*:

*When Winter muffles up his cloak,*
*And binds the mire like a rock;*
*When to the loughs the curlers flock,*
*Wi' gleesome speed,*
*Wha will they station at the cock,*
*Tam Samson's dead?*

Rules were not standardised until 1838 when the Grand Caledonian Curling Club was set up to oversee the game. Queen Victoria saw a demonstration match four years later and promptly gave the organisation the right to call itself the Royal Caledonian Curling Club.

Traditionally, the game was played outdoors in Scotland, on frozen lakes. However, it moved indoors with the invention of artificial ice. The first Scottish rink was opened at Crossmyloof in Glasgow in 1907. It can on occasion still be spotted in the open air, although climate change, not to mention health and safety, does make it a rare event. The most famous outdoor event was a challenge match between North and South Scotland held on the frozen Lake of Menteith but it has not been played since 1979.

The special stones are made of granite and only come from one of two sources – the Ailsa Craig, an uninhabited island in the Firth of Clyde, and the Welsh Trefor Quarry. Granite can only be harvested from the Ailsa at certain times and one company has the sole rights – Kays of Scotland, based in Mauchline, Ayrshire – who supply the curling stones for the Winter Olympics.

*Curling stones*

## SKIMMING WORLD

*The world stone-skimming championships take place every year on a Scottish island. The first event was held on Easdale Island near Oban in Argyllshire in 1983 but was not replayed until 1997 in order to raise funds for the community group which owns the island.*

*It now regularly draws around 300 contestants from all over the world, taking part in various groups, including one for Ladies and Men Old Tossers for those who are no longer in the first flush of youth.*

*Stones must be local and no more than 7.62 cm (three inches) in diameter, must bounce at least three times although entrants are judged on distance thrown.*

# The Eglinton Tournament
*Rich playboys go jousting*

When Queen Victoria was crowned in 1838, in the so-called Penny Coronation due to the various cuts made to the pomp and circumstance, it was decided that one of the more arcane traditions – that of the Marshalling of the Queen's Knight – be dropped.

This involved a lavish banquet for the aristocracy during which the Monarch's Champion would don full armour and offer to fight anyone who disputed the right to the throne.

Archibald William Montgomery, the Scottish 13th Earl of Eglinton, was especially peeved. He didn't like the Whig government and he adored medieval chivalry. His stepfather, Sir Charles Lamb, would also have played a major role in the proceedings.

A chance remark led to him being pressured into organising a jousting tournament, to be held on his estate near Irvine and Kilwinning in Ayrshire. This full-scale medieval contest would lead to him being accused of aristocratic profligacy and force him to sell off parts of his estate to cover his losses.

Practice sessions were held in London's Regents Park, drawing thousands of spectators. The tourney itself was to be held in August 1839 and earlier that year the Sheriff of Ayr warned that if any fatalities occurred then there would be charges of manslaughter and even murder levelled.

As the three-day festival approached, the towns surrounding the Eglinton Estate began to fill up with visitors, brought by train and steamship from Scotland, England and even abroad.

In all, 10,000 tickets were issued but they say ten times that amount crammed into the estate grounds in the shadow of the stately castle to watch 13 knights battle it out. They gathered in fine weather at the start but a storm blew in from the sea. Everyone – Knights, horses, retinue, spectators – was drenched. The plans began to fall apart. Certain traditions initially planned to be adhered to were either dropped

*The Eglinton Tournament*

or forgotten about. The jousting arena swiftly turned into a welter of mud.

When the jousting began, Eglinton himself acquitted himself well but that's more than can be said for some of his friends.

However, the marquee for the grand banquet was washed out. Some of the lucky guests were invited to a smaller affair within the castle, where Prince Louis Napoleon, who would become Emperor Napoleon III of France, displayed his skill in hand-to-hand combat.

The weather continued to be foul and the events for the next day were cancelled. However, on the third day, the sun shone and everything seemed to go more or less as planned. The parade was colourful, the field of play – the lists – were thronged, the jousts were entertaining and the delayed banquet was a success.

The champion was a Captain Fairlie but Eglinton himself received the honours to make up for all the trouble he had experienced. He was given a magnificent eight foot tall silver trophy with carved knights standing on a splendidly carved wooden plinth.

Eglinton had to foot much of the bill himself as his rich friends backed out one-by-one as costs mounted. No-one knows exactly how much he had to spend, certainly many thousands of pounds, and parts of the estate had to be sold off to cover the debt. Eventually the family lost what was left.

Only a tower and parts of wall remain of what was once their magnificent castle, the estate now a country park. The trophy still exists and there is a bridge on the estate, known as the Tournament Bridge, but this wasn't constructed until after the event.

## A GAME OF UPPIES AND DOONIES

*Orkney has its own special football game. The Kirkwall Ba' is played on Christmas Day and New Year's Day and sees two teams – the Uppies and the Doonies – take to the streets to battle for possession of a leather ball filled with cork.*

*To win, the Uppies must touch the ball to a wall on the south side of the island's capital while the Doonies have to get it into the water of Kirkwall Bay. It is a free-for-all rugby-style match, but good-natured. However, that doesn't stop traders in the streets from making sure their premises are well protected the night before.*

# The invention that made the world say Hoy!
*But who came up with it?*

Cycling has become a popular sport around the world, as well as an ideal way of keeping fit – and green – while travelling.

However, the victories of Sir Chris Hoy and Sir Bradley Wiggins et al would not have been possible were it not for a Scotsman. The question is, which Scotsman was it?

Kirkpatrick MacMillan (1812–1878) was born near Thornhill and, after a time working in the iron foundries of Glasgow, eventually joined his father in the smithy trade.

One day he saw a hobbyhorse near his home. Also known as a dandy horse, it was a contraption on which the rider pushed himself along on his feet. This was at a time that such wacky vehicles were in vogue. There were already velocipedes, known as boneshakers, which had the pedals on the front wheels but this method of locomotion was hugely inefficient.

It has been claimed that it was MacMillan who fitted cranks, driving rods, a saddle, handlebars and pedals to the dandy horse idea and rode around the tracks and roads of his home for many years.

He managed the 14 miles to Dumfries in an hour and then made a trip to Glasgow in two days. Unfortunately, the story goes, he hit a child in the Gorbals area and was fined five shillings. A newspaper of the day talked of a 'gentleman bestride a velocipede of ingenious design.' The praise was tempered by the comment that 'it will not supersede the railways.'

Researchers have pointed out that, as a blacksmith, MacMillan would not have been deemed a gentleman. MacMillan did not seek fame for his invention, did not even patent it, and allowed another Scot,

*A Scot may have perfected the bicycle*

Gavin Dalzell from Lesmahagow in Lanarkshire, to improve upon it and claim much of the credit.

It was MacMillan's nephew, corn merchant James Johnston, who spearheaded the campaign to have his uncle named as the true inventor.

However, there was a third Scot – Thomas McCall (1834–1904) – who could claim the title of the man who devised the bicycle. He was also a Dumfriesshire man, born in Penpont not far from MacMillan's village, but lived most of his life in Kilmarnock, Ayrshire. His supporters claim that he invented the first rear wheel powered vehicle, which made the steering and motion so much easier.

Money worries meant that McCall allowed MacMillan and his family to claim much of the credit and, in fact, marry two of his designs into one to make the MacMillan prototype.

The replica that he made for MacMillan is on show at the Dumfries Observatory. But was it all McCall's design? Or, as has been suggested, did he simply build it based on MacMillan's specifications?

The waters have further been muddied with claims that men in England, the United States and France also came up with designs for rear-wheel driven, pedal-powered vehicles.

---

**A WHEELY GOOD IDEA**

*It was a Scot who devised another vital part of the bicycle. In 1887, vet John Boyd Dunlop, a native of Dreghorn in Ayrshire but then practising in Belfast, made his son's tricycle ride a more enjoyable experience by inventing the pneumatic tyre. Until then tyres had been solid wood or rubber.*

*Unlike MacMillan, Dunlop patented his invention and, after a number of improvements, it spread its tyre tracks across the world.*

---

# Just not cricket
*When cricket grounds hosted rugby and football*

In 1871, the very first Scotland v England Rugby international was played in Edinburgh.

There had been a match previously, at the Oval Cricket Ground in London, but the lineage of some of the Scots players was doubtful.

The first real rugby football match to be played under association rules took place on the grounds of the Academical Cricket Club in Raeburn Place, Edinburgh on Monday 27 March. The match was a huge success, raising over £200 at the gate, with 4,000 spectators coming up with the shilling (5p) for entry.

The English wore white emblazoned with a red rose. The Scots were in brown with a thistle. The match was ultimately won by the Scots with one try and one goal against England's single try. Back then a try wasn't worth much points-wise, although today it is worth five points. It was, essentially, a means to try for a goal, which was the real winner. Penalties were not part of the game for it was played by gentlemen and, of course, gentlemen do not cheat.

The match ball was later placed on display in a Stockbridge shop window.

One year later it was football's turn to make history. And once again it was played on a cricket pitch. There had been earlier north and south encounters in the beautiful game but, as with the rugby counterpart, they were played in England with players mostly drawn from London. The match, under Football Association rules, was played on St Andrew's Day – 30 November – on the ground of the West of Scotland Cricket Club in Partick, Glasgow. As in Edinburgh the year before, the crowd of 4,000 football fans each paid a shilling to watch the encounter. Demand was such that it caused a 20 minute delay to the kick-off.

The Scots were all from the Glasgow-based Queen's Park club while the English squad was drawn from nine different teams. As has

*A football match in Kingston-Upon-Thames in 1846*

generally been the case since, the Scots wore blue shirts with a lion crest and the English donned white with the triple lion badge. Some of the players wore hats – caps for the English and red cowls, pointed bonnets, for the Scots.

The English captain, Charles Alcock – who was also secretary of the Football Association – had been injured and was unable to play so he donned a deerstalker hat and became a linesman.

In the first half the Scots seemed to have the upper hand but that switched in the second, with the English having it more their own way.

Spectators were impressed by the way the Scottish players worked as a team – not surprising as they were all from the same side. Reports suggest they used skilful passing to counter-act the English preference for dribbling.

During the match, English goalkeeper Robert Barker decided he'd spent enough time between the sticks, so he switched places with striker William Maynard.

Anyone expecting a goal was disappointed, for the match ended on a 0–0 draw, although one Scot's goal was disallowed as it hit the tape that was doubling as a crossbar. There would not be another goalless draw in an England/Scotland match until 1970.

No photographs of the match exist. Over an argument regarding payment, the photographer stalked off. Despite that, the match was a peaceful affair. The violence and disgraceful behaviour of the 1970s and beyond was a long way off.

---

**THE TRYING GAME**
*The first Rugby International was not without its controversy.*

*When it was played, the rules of the game had not yet been standardised and there was debate whether a second Scottish try was permissible as it had been 'knocked-on' by a player. In Scotland that was allowed but not in England. In the end, the umpire decided in Scotland's favour, although they failed to convert. As he later wrote, 'When an umpire is in doubt, I think he is justified in deciding against the side which makes the most noise. They are probably in the wrong.'*

---

# The first world cup
*The Glasgow-born millionaire who loved sport*

The first official FIFA World Cup competition was held in Uruguay in 1930 – but twenty years before a Scottish businessman had organised his own version.

Glasgow-born Sir Thomas Lipton had amassed a fortune with his successful grocery stores, and his famous tea. He was not born to riches but rather built up his own fortune after being a cabin boy, tobacco planter, book-keeper, salesman and a farmhand in the United States. His parents ran a small store in the Gorbals of Glasgow and it was there he began to create his empire, using the power of advertising to build up a chain of stores. Eventually, he moved into tea, bought a plantation and promoted, and priced, the beverage so that it would appeal to low-paid workers.

He was a keen sportsman, particularly in yachting, and was a regular contestant in the Americas Cup, although he never won.

In 1909, he was honoured by Italy and as a way of thanks he came up with the Sir Thomas Lipton Trophy to be used for an international football competition, to be held in Turin.

Invitations were issued to the football associations of England, Germany, Switzerland and Italy. Curiously, given Lipton's roots, not Scotland. However, the English FA declined to take part but somehow a lowly northern club, West Auckland FC, was invited. Made up of miners, many of whom paid their own way, the club represented their country – and won.

The mining squad won again in 1911 and that meant they could keep the ornate silver trophy. However, the two foreign trips had left the small club in debt and the trophy was used as surety against a loan for £40. Many years later, in 1964, the lender allowed the trophy to be returned for £100. It was stolen thirty years later and has never been recovered, although Unilever, who had folded Lipton's Tea into their conglomerate bosom, did furnish a replica.

The story of the underdog miners winning the cup was told in a TV drama, *The Captain's Tale*, starring Dennis Waterman and Andrew Keir as Sir Thomas Lipton.

*Businessman Sir Thomas Lipton was a keen sportsman*

## THE GAME THAT MADE THE RECORD BOOKS

*On a wet day in September 1885, Arbroath FC faced Aberdeen Bon Accord in a first round Scottish Cup tie. The game would become one of the most resounding routs in football history.*

*John 'Jocky' Petrie, an 18-year-old centre forward, scored an amazing 13 goals to help Arbroath to a stunning 36–0 victory against the visitors, who were so new to the game that they didn't have boots or kit. Petrie's feat remained uneclipsed until 2001 when Archie Thompson equalled the tally for Australia against American Samoa.*

*Arbroath's goalkeeper, Jim Milne Snr, had so little to do that he borrowed an umbrella to shield him from the rain.*

## HEADLINE INSPIRATION

*When tiny Inverness Caledonian Thistle, known as Caley Thistle, took on Glasgow Celtic in a Scottish Cup fixture in 2000, they helped create one of the finest ever newspaper headlines.*

*The First Division part-timers faced their mighty opponents at Celtic's Parkhead home and won 3–1, including an own goal by Celtic's Lubomir Moravcik.*

*The surprising victory prompted a moment of genius for a headline writer at the Scottish Sun, who turned to a Mary Poppins song for inspiration when he came up with 'Super Caley go ballistic, Celtic are atrocious.'*

# TALES FROM THE DARK SIDE

Readers of a nervous disposition go no further, for here be killers and monsters and things that go bump in the night.

## The family from hell
*The story of the bloody Beanes*

The story of a family of bloodthirsty cannibals living on the west coast of Scotland is merely a legend. It has even been suggested that the tale was invented by English propagandists to stir up sentiment against the Scots. It first appeared in print in the early 18th century, just as the two nations were forming a union. The name of the patriarch – Sawney – was a derogatory term used in London in print for the Scots.

There is some doubt as to when the events would have taken place – whether in the reign of James I of Scotland (1394–1437) or James VI, James I in England (1566–1625). However, using the mantra of filmmaker John Ford, when the legend becomes fact, print the legend.

Alexander, or Sawney, Beane was born in East Lothian to an honest family. He, though, was not so law-abiding and he teamed up with a woman of similar bent to embark on a life of crime. They moved to the west and settled into a sea cave in what is now present day South Ayrshire.

Over the years the couple bred prodigiously. And their children inter-bred, until they were a fearsome pack of feral creatures who lived by murdering and robbing travellers. But worse, they also turned to cannibalism.

Their cave was an ideal fortress. It ran deep into the land and was a warren of corridors and caverns. When the tide was in no-one could penetrate to their living quarters.

However, after 25 years of bloody depredations, with people mysteriously vanishing off the face of the earth and body parts washing up on the beach, moves were made to dig out the Beane clan, root and branch. The king himself led a force of 500 men to Carrick to hunt down the murderers. Near the entrance to the cave their hunting dogs erupted in a cacophony of barking and howling and their handlers knew they were on a hot scent. They led the searchers through the dank corridors until they reached a vast open cavern. What they found there was horrifying, for this was used as the Beane's larder. They also found a hoard of stolen gold and silver.

And then they found the family, spitting and snarling in the shadows. There was Sawney himself, his wife, eight sons, six daughters, 18 grandsons and 14 granddaughters. They put up a struggle but the King's men were not unwary travellers, they were fighting men, and the family was soon subdued.

The cave was sealed off and the family transported back to Edinburgh where they would be punished. And that punishment was as brutal as the crimes, for the Beanes did not die an easy death. They were defiant to the last, for they vented 'the most dreadful imprecations until the very last gasp of life.'

The story has influenced writers and film makers over the years. Author S.R. Crockett used it in his adventure *The Grey Man*, a rollicking tale about the feud among the Kennedy family, known as the Kings of Carrick. Film Director Wes Craven said he was inspired by the story to write his gory horror *The Hills Have Eyes*, while a low-budget modernised version was made in 2013 with Scottish actor David Hayman. Sawney and his family are also an attraction for tourists in the popular

*A family of cannibals were reputed to live on the Ayrshire coast*

Edinburgh Dungeon.

The cave in which the Beanes were reputed to have lived for so long is said to be at Bennane Head near Ballantrae. Other sites have been suggested but this is the favourite.

---

**THE KILLER BUTCHER**

*The story of Sawney Beane may have been inspired by an earlier case-cum-legend about Christie Cleek and his accomplices.*

*Andrew Christie was a butcher who turned robber in the Highlands during the 14th century. During a particularly harsh period of famine he used his old skills to butcher a dead body to feed the gang. They then developed a liking for human flesh and Christie used a hook on a long pole, known as a Cleek, to haul his victims to the ground.*

*Eventually the gang was hunted down and killed but their leader, now called Christie Cleek, supposedly escaped and lived a quiet life in the lowlands.*

---

# The glen of weeping
*The atrocity at Glencoe*

Entering Glencoe from the south is an awesome experience. Buachaille Etive More – the Great Herdsman of Etive – looms at the entrance to the glen like a sentry and the mountains crowd around the narrow road, water bleeding like open wounds from streams and fissures. It is impressive in all weathers but it is when the mist clings to the ridges and tops of the three mountains – Buachaille Etive More, Buachaille Etive Beag (the Little Shepherd of Etive) and Bidean nam Bian, with its Three Sisters – that you feel its history land upon you. It was here, in 1692, that an act of such barbarity occurred that it has instilled horror and revulsion through the centuries.

The MacDonalds of Glencoe were accomplished cattle thieves, and their skill had them dubbed 'The Gallow's Herd.'

In 1691, King William of Orange declared an amnesty to all Highlands chiefs who had fought for the ousted James II – as long as they declared their allegiance to him before the year was ended.

By December only MacIain of Glencoe held out but on 31 December he set off for Fort William to swear the oath. Once there he was told that it could only be taken at Inverary, 60 miles away. Further delays meant that MacIain was six days over the deadline before he took the oath. However, he made his way back home being told that the authorities would be assured that the Highland clans had all fallen into line.

The MacDonalds of Glencoe were not loved. Secretary of State Sir John Dalrymple of Stair saw them as 'the worst in all the Highlands' and wanted steps taken to 'root out this damnable sept.' It was, he wrote, a 'great work of charity.'

The man charged with handling the assignment was Captain Robert Campbell of Glenlyon, whose lands had suffered at the hands of the MacDonalds but who lost everything through his own

*Signal Rock in Glencoe, where a beacon was lit to begin the slaughter*

gambling and drinking. He arrived on 1 February with a force of 120 men and was given shelter, as Highland hospitality demanded, by MacIain. The soldiers were billeted there for ten days, eating, sleeping and drinking with the families in the village.

Then, on 12 February, the fatal order came. Captain Campbell was to *'put all to the sword under 70. You are to have special care that the old fox and his sons do on no account escape your hands…'*

The massacre was horrific. MacIain was shot in his bed, his wife abused and the rings torn from her fingers. Families were gunned down or bayoneted. The snow was stained with blood. Two officers resigned their commission on the spot and refused to take part. Other soldiers were said to have tried to warn the families.

By the end of that bloody night 38 MacDonalds – men, women and children – had been murdered. Others had fled into the mountains. A few died in the snow.

A London journalist later heard of the massacre and brought it into the public eye. The King denied seeing, or signing, the order, which was possible as he was wont to let papers build up to such a degree that he signed them all too quickly, with little attention to their content. The Master of Stair was forced to resign but he was not gone long from the corridors of power.

Captain Campbell drank himself to death and was buried in a pauper's grave in Belgium.

## Bloody deeds and bloody shirts
*A battle in 1603 led to a clan being outlawed*

The battle of Glen Fruin in 1603 was fought between the MacGregors, backed by their allies, and the Colquhouns and Buchanans, who were supported by James VI. The MacGregors had earlier been recruited by the Campbell Chief to help him seize land from the Colquhouns. There was little love between their two clans but the wily Campbell needed someone to blame if his plan failed.

*Warfare was a way of life for the clansman*

They raided the Colquhoun lands around Luss on the banks of Loch Lomond and carried off what booty they could.

The Colquhoun laird knew that Campbell was behind it but was not prepared to accuse him – he was a powerful man and was Justice General, to boot. Colquhoun complained bitterly to King James VI, demanding that he issue a letter of 'Fire and Sword' against the MacGregors, who responded by sending another force, this time to Glen Fruin. Four hundred MacGregors battled with an enemy double their number and emerged victorious, claiming they slaughtered 200 of the enemy.

However, the Colqhouns sent women with the bloody shirts of their husbands to drive their point home to the king. James, furious that the side he favoured had been so royally routed, passed an Act that made it legal to 'extirpit Clan Gregor and ruit out their posterities and name.' In other words, the MacGregors were outlawed and were fair game.

To this day, MacGregors claim it was all a fit up, the battle was fair, and the grieving widows were, in fact, prostitutes waving shirts stained with sheep's blood. However, they were forced further into the Highlands where their raiding and robbery earned them the nickname 'Children of the Mist.'

## DEATH AND THE MAIDEN

*Scotland had its own version of the guillotine long before the heads began to fall in the French Revolution.*

*The beheading device was called 'The Maiden', perhaps after* **mod-dun,** *place of execution. It was introduced after James Douglas, Earl of Morton, reputedly witnessed a similar machine, the Halifax Gibbet, at work. Legend has it he was also the first to feel its sting but in reality it was Tom Scott, one of the conspirators in the murder of Mary Queen of Scot's secretary David Rizzio. Morton, later Regent, was executed for his part in the murder of Mary's husband, Lord Darnley.*

# The judge's wife
*To protect himself, his Lordship had his wife kidnapped*

In 1732, the then Lord of Session, James Erskine, Lord Grange, informed friends and acquaintances that his dear wife, Rachel Chiesly, had died.

*Lady Grange was hidden away by her husband*

The marriage had been stormy. He was a powerful advocate, then judge, and a Presbyterian with Jacobite leanings. She was beautiful and headstrong and fond of a good time. They only married in the first place because he got her pregnant.

It was her drinking, temper and alleged streak of madness that struck fear into his Lordship's heart, for there was always the danger that she might let slip a secret or two regarding his secret meetings with Highlanders with a yen to see the Stuarts back on the throne.

Even after their separation, thanks to his infidelities, Lord Grange worried her loose lips would sink his ship. What was worse, she had a letter which proved his treason and she had made it clear she was none-too-fond of her philandering

husband. And so her death was announced.

There was grieving, there was a funeral, with his Lordship walking behind the bier weeping like a grieving husband.

The problem was, reports of her Ladyship's death were greatly exaggerated. She had, in fact, been spirited away under the orders of her estranged husband, who had some of his more ruthless Highland friends break into her home in Edinburgh.

She was taken to Glencoe, then Loch Hourn in Knoydart, on the west coast. Finally, she was shipped off to barren St Kilda where she survived for seven years in the most basic of accommodation – a stone hut – with no provisions being sent to her and totally dependent on a local minister for shelter. Finally, though, a letter got through to Edinburgh but before she could be rescued she was snatched away again, eventually being held in Skye, where she died, still a captive, in 1745.

No action was ever taken against her husband, who had resigned his position and stood as an MP. Still womanising and fond of a drink himself, he died in 1754.

## CORPSES ON TRIAL

*The Earl of Huntly died of a heart attack on a battlefield in 1562. Nevertheless, his corpse was embalmed in vinegar, aquae vitae and other substances and taken to Edinburgh where the dead man was charged with treason against Mary, Queen of Scots and his lands declared forfeit to the Crown.*

*The corpses of two Scots nobles accused of treason were placed on trial and then ritually executed. John, Earl of Gowrie, and his brother Alexander Ruthven were part of an alleged conspiracy in 1600 to murder King James VI. Although they were killed on the spot, their bodies were preserved for trial after which they were hung, drawn and quartered.*

# The Ripper Connection
*Dundee killer's final confession*

In April 1889, a man called William Henry Bury was hanged in Dundee for the brutal murder of his wife, Ellen. Bury had actually confessed to the police, at first claiming that she had committed suicide.

*William Henry Bury*

Wolverhampton-born Bury, an alcoholic, and his wife had recently arrived from London, where he had earned a living selling sawdust. He was known to be violent, especially towards his wife. He cheated his way into rooms in the city's Princes Street and then set to drinking as much as he could in local pubs, often leaving his wife in the cold, bare flat. But sometimes they went out together, as in the last night of her life.

The last anyone saw of Ellen Bury was when she left a pub with her husband. There was a scream in the night, then no more. Bury told friends that his wife was ill and had taken to her bed. Eventually he made his way to a police station and claimed that his wife had killed herself with a rope (that he was known to have bought) and he had then stabbed her and placed her in a trunk. He could not explain why he committed such an atrocity, although reports say he either exclaimed, 'I am Jack the Ripper' or 'I am a Jack the Ripper.'

There were further links to the notorious Whitechapel murders in the flat. Chalked on a wall leading to the flat were the words *Jack the Ripper is at the back of this door.* Further on police found the legend *Jack the Ripper is in this sellar.* No one can say for certain who wrote those words but it can be assumed it was Bury himself. Or perhaps his wife. It should be noted that messages on walls formed a portion of the Ripper slayings in London.

He was found guilty of his wife's murder and executed on 24 April, 1889.

So was he Jack the Ripper? Some writers seem satisfied that he was, others less so. Certainly he was in London's East End at the time of the killings and they stopped once he moved to Scotland. He was deranged and violent. The method of murder was different but still involved strangling and mutilation. London police remained unconvinced that he was nothing more than a wife murderer.

However, it is said that he made a detailed confession to the Whitechapel murders, with many astonishing revelations, which was sent to the Home Secretary of the day. That confession, if it ever existed, has never been made public.

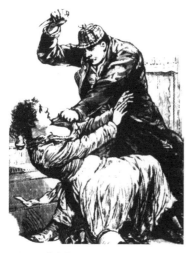

*Was a wife killer in Dundee Jack the Ripper?*

# INDEX

Amazing and Extraordinary
Facts: Ireland
Sarah Elliott
ISBN: 978-1-910821-13-8

Amazing and Extraordinary
Facts: London
Stephen Halliday
ISBN: 978-1-910821-02-2

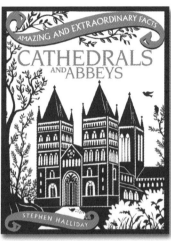

Amazing and Extraordinary
Facts: Cathedrals and Abbeys
Stephen Halliday
ISBN: 978-1-910821-04-6

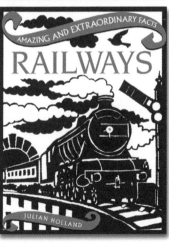

Amazing and Extraordinary
Facts: Railways
Julian Holland
ISBN: 978-1-910821-00-8

For more great books visit our website at **www.rydonpublishing.co.uk**

# THE AUTHOR

Glasgow-born Douglas Skelton is a former journalist and local newspaper editor. He has published 11 non-fiction books dealing with true crime and the darker side of Scottish history as well as six crime novels. His novel, *Open Wounds,* was nominated for the McIlvanney Award in 2016. He lives in Ayrshire.

# AUTHOR ACKNOWLEDGEMENTS

With thanks to all at Rydon Publishing as well as Linda MacFadyen and my Crime Factor colleagues Neil Broadfoot, Gordon Brown and Mark Leggatt.

# PICTURE CREDITS